Anointed or Annoying?

Searching for the Fruit of Revival

Anointed or Annoying?

Searching for the Fruit of Revival

Ken Gott

Revival Press

An Imprint of
Destiny Image_® Publishers, Inc.
P.O. Box 310
Shippensburg, PA 17257-0310

ISBN 0-7684-1003-7

For Worldwide Distribution
Printed in the U.S.A.

This book and all other Destiny Image, Revival Press, and Treasure House books are available at Christian bookstores and distributors worldwide.

For a U.S. bookstore nearest you, call **1-800-722-6774**.
For more information on foreign distributors, call **717-532-3040**.
Or reach us on the Internet: **http://www.reapernet.com**

Dedication

This book is dedicated to Herbert Harrison, my father-in-law, my mentor, and my friend, who passed into the direct presence of the Lord on October 10, 1997.

Endorsements

Ken Gott is a man who has been powerfully touched by this new move of the Holy Spirit. His ministry has exploded on the international scene as a result of many months and years of nightly meetings in his own church in Sunderland, England. He is a dear friend and a very anointed preacher indeed.

—John Arnott
Senior Pastor, Toronto Airport Christian Fellowship

Ken Gott's account of his journey in personal renewal is a "must read" for anyone who is sincerely seeking a fresh encounter with the Holy Spirit. As I read his book, I was reminded of John the Baptist's words concerning his relationship to the Messiah: "This is the assigned moment for Him to move into the center, while I slip off to the sidelines" (Jn. 3:30, The Message). The true key to spiritual success, Ken tells us, is to do what John did.

—Joseph L. Garlington
Pastor of Covenant Church of Pittsburgh

Surprisingly honest, at times just funny, Ken Gott gets to the heart of the reader, the Church, and revival. You will find it difficult to put down this book.

—Gerald Coates
Speaker, Author, and Broadcaster

Hazel and I were invited to minister at Ken and Lois Gott's fledgling church in Sunderland about ten years ago. I prophesied that the church would experience a great revival, and that people would come from around the world to take part in it. The Gotts have graphically described in this book the amazing work of the Holy Spirit to bring them to the place where they could be true instruments of revival. They have been marvelously guided step by step and through their obedience have witnessed one of England's greatest outpourings of the Spirit in this century. I recommend this book as necessary reading for Christians who are longing for a Heaven-sent revival.

—Frank Houston
Senior Minister of Sydney Christian Life Centre

Contents

Foreword

Some time ago a minister friend, Pastor Cleddie Keith of Heritage Fellowship Assembly of God in Florence, Kentucky, invited me to preach a conference at his church. He told me that I would be sharing the pulpit with a preacher from England by the name of Ken Gott. Ken Gott was pastoring in Sunderland, England, and was experiencing a major revival that had continued for several years. Cleddie Keith said that God led him to bring together what he called "the two fountainheads of revival" from Europe and America to be merged. Little did any of us know what a union it would be. Since that time, Ken and his wife Lois and my wife Brenda and I have been bonded as very close personal friends as well as proponents of this last-day move of God. I will ever be thankful to my good friend Cleddie Keith for being the visionary that he is.

I admire Ken Gott's ability to take the most simple truths and make them profound. It is a gift that many of us in the ministry desire. Ken is a wordsmith who can take something that all of us take for granted in Scripture and, after he has put his touch to it, make it unforgettable.

Ken resides in Sunderland, England, which is well-known worldwide as the home base for God's generals through the years. It's no wonder, for Ken himself has been used by God through his integrity and good name to help spread revival over all the earth. When you hear Ken preach on revival or share his powerful testimony, you know that you have heard from a legitimate voice. In the Kingdom of God there are many echoes, but very few voices. Ken Gott is a voice that God is using to make the peoples of the earth hungry for more of Him.

I remember down through the years of reading authors whose books had a powerful impact on me. As I would cull my library from time to time, there were certain books that I would set aside as special. I have kept a few books in my ministry that I refuse to let go of. This book will be one of those special ones. Once you take it in, you won't let it go.

John A. Kilpatrick, Pastor
Brownsville Assembly of God

Chapter 1

Making Room

When John Arnott of Toronto Airport Christian Fellowship said, "I'd like to pray for you," my response was, "Well, that would be wonderful." And I gently pushed my wife, Lois, in front of me. As he prayed for her, I watched Lois do things I'd never, ever, seen her do before.

Although no one was touching her, she bounced up and down like a puppet on a string until she finally collapsed in a heap on the floor. "Has she ever done this before?" John asked. I just shook my head and said, "No, she's never done *that* before." Now, I would know if she'd done that. Yes sir, I would definitely know, and she has *never*, ever, done that before.

Then John said, "I'd like to pray for you now." I was uncertain, wondering if I would do the things that my wife had just done. John Arnott moved his great big hand toward me until it rested right on top of my head, and the moment it landed I saw a vision.

I'm not big on dreams and visions. I know some people who get them all the time. They hear audible voices, get caught up to Heaven, receive open visions, and recall everything in

Dolby sound and Technicolor. Normally I don't get any of those things, but on that day in Toronto, Ontario, it was my turn. That in itself was a miracle. Until then I had actively discouraged anyone in my church from attending conferences where John Wimber or other key Vineyard leaders were speaking, and Vineyard music was out of the question. Toronto Airport Christian Fellowship still retained the full flavor and ministry style of the Vineyard churches with which it had been associated for years.

That was all forgotten in that moment. I was so excited that I shouted, "I can see it! I can see it! I can see it!" John Arnott asked, "Well, what can you see, Ken?" At first I thought he was really rude. Why was he talking to me while I was having such a great spiritual experience? (I didn't know you could do that, you see. I wasn't "Vineyard trained." It was a completely new experience for me.) That's why I just ignored him.

As he prayed for me, I closed my eyes, and I could see Moses' burning bush. Then I saw one after another springing up until they were multiplied 100 times and more. Suddenly I saw them coming together as one big blazing fire. It seemed like the Holy Spirit overlaid a map or template of Britain, my nation, right on top of the fires and the wilderness. The fires were clustered in northeast England, with my hometown of Sunderland right in the middle.

Then it seemed as though I felt the Lord put His hands inside me and pull. I know it sounds odd, but I literally felt like my spirit man was being *stretched* by God. Now I was really glad we were in the aisle (or corridor, as we call them). I bent over at the waist with my arms extended out to the side in an exaggerated way—I'd never done anything like that in my life. Then I moaned with a loud voice, "O-h-h-h-h, o-h-h-h-h."

Spirit Man in a Growth Spurt

I felt my spirit man stretch and stretch within the confines of my physical body. It was my spirit man in a growth spurt. I'd limited my inward man so much that I'd kept him unnaturally small. This supernatural expansion process was physically painful! The best way I can describe it is to say that I felt like the American comic book and television character called the Incredible Hulk. What was inside me was bigger than my body or clothing. I was expanding with explosive power, and I felt like God was stretching me, giving me a greater capacity to receive more of what He was doing.

I sometimes joke about being a third generation Pentecostal Assemblies of God man, and wisecrack, "If ever a man needed deliverance...." The truth is that I have received an incredibly rich inheritance from my spiritual cradle, and I am still an Assemblies of God minister. Yet, as with any upbringing, I had also discovered that I had inherited some built-in limitations.

I had limited the Holy Spirit to speaking in tongues, interpretation, and the odd prophecy that might come along. That was the way I was trained, and that was all I had experienced. I was sure that any time the Holy Spirit showed up, one of those three things would happen (and little else). My spirit man had been squeezed and contained so he could fit into that box. Then I found myself in "that Toronto place" that was so controversial, and the Lord sovereignly planted me into a bigger place. It was almost as if my spirit man said, "Wow, I'm going to grow into this expanded man."

At the turn of the century, my hometown of Sunderland was the site of a revival that birthed the Pentecostal movement in Britain. It wasn't huge by today's standards, but the results of that revival were significant. A born-again plumber and soulwinner by the name of Smith Wigglesworth traveled a great distance to attend the Sunderland meetings, hoping to receive the baptism of the Holy Spirit. After days of frustration, on his way out of town, he decided to stop at the house of Alexander Boddy, the evangelical Anglican vicar of All Saints Parish Church, who was leading the revival.

Vicar Boddy wasn't there, but his wife was. She agreed to pray for Smith, and so it was there in Mrs. Boddy's kitchen that the great Smith Wigglesworth was baptized in the Holy Ghost and fire "at the hands of a woman" on October 28, 1907. (That should jar some traditions right there.) Considering what happened in Smith's life after that, I'd say that revival was worth it, wouldn't you? Smith Wigglesworth so hungered after God that he traveled many hours to attend a revival in a distant town in search of "more."

Despite frustration and apparent failure, he humbled himself to try one more time before going home. He didn't mind kneeling in a kitchen to receive prayer from a minister's wife—he was making room for the world-changing gift that God wanted to deposit in him.

Make Room—No Matter the Cost

I felt much better about my "Incredible Hulk" experience in Toronto when I remembered that Wigglesworth used to say he felt ten times bigger on the inside than he did on the outside because his spirit man was ten times larger than his natural man. Judging by his track record, we know that Smith Wigglesworth expanded, enlarged, reorganized, and increased his capacity to receive whatever God wanted to send him. He made room no matter the cost.

When you prepare the place in your heart, the Holy Spirit will grow into it. And let me tell you right now that you can't prepare a place that is too big for the Holy Spirit to fill. The Bible tells us that one day the whole earth will be filled with the knowledge of God's glory (see Hab. 2:14).

*Now it happened one day that Elisha went to Shunem, where there was a notable woman, and she persuaded him to eat some food. So it was, as often as he passed by, he would turn in there to eat some food. And she said to her husband, "Look now, I know that this is a holy man of God, who passes by us regularly. Please, **let us make a small upper room** on the wall; and let us put a bed for him there, and a table and a chair and a lampstand; so it will be, whenever he comes to us, he can turn in there." And it happened one day that he came there, and he turned in to the upper room and lay down there (2 Kings 4:8-11).*

Of all the people whom Elisha the prophet dealt with, one woman was singled out because she *made room* for God (in the form of Elisha, God's man for that day). This woman was perceptive, noble, wise, hospitable, and very persuasive. The Bible says she "persuaded" Elisha to stop by her house for a meal. The Hebrew word for persuaded, *chazaq*, means "to fasten upon; hence to seize, be strong, obstinate; to bind, restrain, conquer."[1]

Is Your House Irresistible to God?

This woman just wouldn't take "no" for an answer. Evidently she was a great cook and hostess though, because from then on her house became Elisha's oasis. He couldn't seem to pass through there without stopping for a meal. Is your house irresistible to God? Do you lay such a good table and provide such a warm reception for Him that He can't bear to pass by you without stopping in for a meal and some fellowship?

The Shunammite woman recognized what was going on with Elisha. In the Old Testament, the Holy Spirit hadn't been poured out on all flesh yet. God only worked through a few individuals, and at times only one. Elisha the prophet was the point man for God's power and authority in his day. In other words, the whole move of God for that day was personified in the prophet Elisha.

This woman had enough perception to understand that Elisha was not an ordinary man. He spoke as one who spoke the Word of the Lord; he did things that other men didn't do. She was willing to reorganize her home, inconvenience herself, restructure, and make room to accommodate the prophet. We need to do likewise in relation to this present move of God.

This Shunammite woman was a thinker and a planner. She wasn't happy with her new status quo. She wanted to do *more* than serve God's man a light lunch when he was in the neighborhood. She told her husband, "Let's expand for the man of God. Why don't we make him a room so he'll do more than eat with us once a month—maybe he'll even stay with us for a weekend or a month or a year." She totally reorganized her house. She restructured it to make room for the move of God in her time.

I don't want God to just turn up at "ministry time" in a standard Sunday service. I want to make it so comfortable for the Lord that He'll want to be there all the time! This lady knew how to make a simple room into a home. She went out and picked out a comfortable bed, and she bought some matching furniture and a lampstand. If she had lived in our day, I imagine that Elisha would have enjoyed his own bath and shower, his own TV (sanctified, of course), and maybe even his own parking space for the donkeys and camels. This woman wanted God's man to stay in her house 24 hours a day, and she wanted him to do his praying *in her house*. If Elisha talked to God from her spare room, then God would know her address and her phone number too. She wanted to make it so comfortable that Elisha wouldn't even think of passing by her house to stay at a better place.

That is exactly what we did in Sunderland upon our return from Toronto. We did not expect God to turn up in our structures and programs; rather, we totally reorganized to accommodate Him. Look at places like Pensacola or Toronto that are housing a move of God. They are totally willing to abandon their own plans to accommodate God in their house.

"And it happened one day that he came there, and he turned in to the upper room and lay down there" (2 Kings 4:11). If you want God's Presence to dwell with you, then I encourage you to *make room*, expand, reorganize, and even reconsider your programs.

If you are a pastor or Christian leader, you may have tried to add this move of God on to your own plans and structures and then wondered why God does not stay in your house. I encourage you to make yourself so flexible and accommadating that, no matter when God shows up, He is comfortable enough to stay if He so chooses.

As leaders, we can be so sure that God will bless our plans that we totally fail to instantly reorganize for Him. We have to make room for God in our thinking, in our methodology, and in our faith and courage. We must make room and expand to receive more of Him.

A Holy Ghost Setup

In June of 1994, only a few weeks before Lois and I went to Toronto, a friend named Wes Richards phoned me and said, "Ken, I'm taking my ministry team to Holy Trinity Brompton, an Anglican church in London, because the Holy Ghost has fallen there. Now, we believe this is a visitation of God, Ken. I've put off phoning you for two days, but I've been prompted by the Lord continually. I resisted it all along, and I thought, 'This is crazy!' But Ken, our whole team feels that you should be with us."

An Anglican church in London was the last place I ever wanted to be. After all, I was a dyed-in-the-wool Pentecostal Assemblies of God man. Pridefully I wondered, *What could the Anglicans possibly know about the Holy Spirit?*

After all, aren't we Pentecostals the ones who "own" the Holy Spirit? We know our doctrine, don't we? Weren't we the ones who tarried for the baptism of the Holy Spirit when everyone else wanted to bury it? Weren't we the ones who got out there on a limb? We embraced the "full gospel" and went through all the bad times of ridicule and persecution, but now that it is "respectable," it seems like everybody wants to jump on the bandwagon.

I know that sounds pretty sour, but that was my attitude. I made up my mind that I was not going to go down to any stuffy Anglican liturgical service. That left me with only one alternative—to stall and avoid commitment. I thought, *Look, Wes, it's a five-hour drive to London from here. I don't think I can do it. That Anglican meeting starts at 11:00, so I would have to leave really early in the morning. I don't feel like I want to take a train.* Then I got a bright idea that I thought was relatively safe. I thought to myself, *I'm willing to fly down. If there's a ticket, I'll come down.* "Okay, Wes," I said, "let me check on some things and I'll get back to you." (Of course, I was sure that no tickets would be available for the next day.)

I'd forgotten one very important factor in all of this: God wanted me there! Lois phoned British Airways, and I was shocked when she said the ticket agent had one ticket left. I should have sensed it—this was a *Holy Ghost setup.* And Lois didn't help any. She told me in her usual non-coercive way, "Ken, I *really* feel you should go." On top of everything else, the Lord had already supplied half of the cost of the airline ticket through a gift from a church member.

The very next morning, I found myself standing in this Anglican church. Everything was unfamiliar and uncomfortable to me. There was a baptismal font as well as an altar rail. There were those famous stained glass windows, soaring ceilings, and pews. All of us "Holy Ghost men" were bunched together on the back row. Things were about to get worse.

The vicar, Sandy Millar, greeted the relatively small group of 130 or so ministers at that service and then meekly said, "We'll start with a time of worship, if that's alright?" I thought, *You don't lead a meeting like that!* Then a man stood up with a guitar and began singing Vineyard songs. Now if there was one thing I really did not like, it was Vineyard music.

God Had "Checked It Out"

The problem was that I had sensed the presence of God right in the midst of everything I disliked. (One of the good things from my Pentecostal heritage was that I did have a basic appreciation for God's Presence.) I stood in the row thinking, *Well, if God has checked it out, then it must be all right. I can tell He's here.*

Once we got through the Vineyard music (which I love today), Bishop David Pytches, the vicar of St. Andrews Anglican Church in Chorleywood, told us what would happen when the Holy Spirit came upon us. (That really irked me.

We knew what would happen! We would speak in tongues, for goodness' sake.) He said, "Some of you may laugh, and some may fall to the floor. Some of you will find yourselves doing all kinds of things that you have never done before."

The whole time, my professional Pentecostal mind was saying, *No, they don't do that. They speak in tongues, that's all they do.*

Then the bishop stood at the front of the church and said, "Now we are going to have a ministry time." A "ministry time"? What was that? He explained that "ordinary" people from the congregation were going to pray for us! *No, they are not,* I thought. "Let us pray," he said.

(I don't know what you know about genuine "Pentecostal prayers," but they are *supposed* to be loud, because everybody knows God hears loud prayers better than soft prayers. And seasoned Pentecostal professionals are trained to emphasize words for more power and effectiveness. I suppose our theological position has been that it makes it easier for God to hear our prayers and accurately gauge our faith that way.)

That Will Get You Nowhere!

Well, this man didn't know any of that vital information. He just stood at the front, meekly lifted his hands, and prayed in a very soft, very polite English accent, "Come, Holy Spirit."

I looked at him and thought, *Now that will get you nowhere. God didn't even hear that.* Two seconds later, that solemn Anglican church sanctuary was in an uproar. There were people doing all the things that the bishop had told us they would do! I had to close my eyes. I just couldn't bear to look for long. I was thinking, *Oh, God help us.*

Then I felt a nudge in my ribs. One of my friends leaned over and said, "Ken, I think I have just heard from God. We need to humble ourselves and go down to the front to ask the bishop to pray for us." I looked at him and thought, *You have to be joking!* I didn't have to open my mouth; he could read my mind. He just looked at me and said, "Okay, if you're not going, we are." And off they went. You know what happened, don't you? I promptly crumbled under peer pressure and reluctantly began to follow them.

When our group finally reached the front, Wes Richards said to the bishop, "We want all God has to offer." He may as well have said, "We're Pentecostals, and we need God." I was thinking, *Now he didn't have to say that! Why couldn't Wes have said, "We're a little bit dry. We just need a bit of refreshing,"* you know? This was a bit tough on my Pentecostal ego. It was about to get even worse.

Then Bishop Pytches said, "Okay, hold hands and form a circle." Immediately I resisted. Well, where is that in the Bible, for goodness' sake? I mean, Pentecostal men of God do not form circles. They just don't do that. But we did.

So there we were, five Pentecostal men of faith and power, holding hands like children in a circle, at an Anglican altar. Then this Anglican bishop prayed a second prayer that was worse than the first one! If you have a pen and paper, then you might want to write this one down. All he said was, "Father, come and get them. Come and get them." Predictably, I had a solid response to that: *What kind of prayer is that?* I was not impressed.

Two seconds later I was *very impressed.* I spent the next one and a half hours on my back, under the font of an Anglican church with my Pentecostal friends. It was like the Holy Spirit had dropped a bomb in the middle of our circle. Not only were we on our backs, but we also managed to shed every shred of dignity! We were laughing uncontrollably. We were getting absolutely falling-down drunk. One time I looked up to see the baptismal font overhead and I started laughing. (*I don't even believe in that!* I thought, and laughed all the more.)

The Anglican bishop suddenly hovered over me again. Even though my eyes were closed at the time, I could sense his presence. I reluctantly opened my eyes and thought, *Oh God, he's looking at me.* I couldn't believe it. He bent over, reached out with his hand, drew the cross on my forehead, and said, "I bless you with the cross of Christ." (I sometimes joke that he couldn't resist taking advantage once he got one of those stubborn Pentecostals down on the floor in a helpless position.)

Sealed by the Bishop

When I acknowledged that God was using this Anglican man as His chosen instrument, I felt the Holy Ghost begin a major work of transformation in my heart. I knew that God wanted me to break out of my rigid religious box and accept the whole Body of Christ. He wants us all to understand that He never called other believers to conform to *us*. They are called to be conformed to *Christ*, and Him alone. If we want to see God's "entrustments" (those unique and precious things entrusted only to us) worked out in our lives, then we've got to accept the many diverse members of the Body of Christ as they are and walk in unity of spirit. The people of God were not made in our image, but in God's image.

My attitude that morning had become disarmingly simple: "That man is full of the Holy Ghost, so if that's the way he blesses people, that's fine." I loved it! Anglican after Anglican laid their hands on us and blessed us in Jesus' name.

I have to tell you that I love the Anglican Church today. I love it. In fact, every Friday night for many weeks an Anglican evangelist named J. John conducted a revival meeting with us in our church! He's known as the "British Billy Graham," and together we ministered to hundreds of Anglican leaders in Bishop Pytches' old church in May, 1997. Every one of those Anglicans was hungry and thirsty for God!

On the way home from London I was still thanking God that none of my congregation was there to see me rolling all over that Anglican church like a falling-down drunk. I remember saying to the Lord, "Was it totally necessary for me to roll around for an hour and a half in front of that Anglican church, right under the baptismal font? And why did I have to laugh uncontrollably?"

The Lord just ignored my questions and asked me another: "Ken, how is your heart?" That made me pause for a moment. I said, "Lord, do You know what? My heart feels great! In fact, it hasn't felt this good for a long, long time." In a moment I realized that my driven, performance-oriented heart that was full of pride, had been changed. I had fallen passionately in love with the Lord Jesus Christ all over again. It was like being born again, again. Then the Lord asked me this: "How would you like your people to feel like you're feeling right now?" I answered without hesitation, "Lord, I'd love for them to feel this."

It was logical to assume that if I was so driven to perform and win acceptance from others, then many of the people in my congregation were probably very driven and performance-oriented as well. One of the time-honored axioms of leadership says, "As the leaders are, so the people are." I wanted my congregation to feel as I did now. Then the Lord gave me a strategy to bring this to pass, a plan that literally had nothing to do with me at all. All I had to do was know how to operate a cassette tape machine.

We had suspended our Sunday evening services for the summer. So I called a special Sunday night meeting in an upper room and met about 100 people who responded. Then I played a half-hour tape of a pastor's wife from London named Ellie Mumford. It was a recording of her testimony given to the church at Holy Trinity Brompton, in which she described her experiences in Toronto. (It was after Ellie gave her simple, straightforward testimony that God began to pour out His Spirit on the Anglican congregation there.)

They Wanted to Make More Room

At the conclusion of the cassette tape, I prayed the most humbling prayer I've ever prayed: "Come, Holy Spirit." I didn't shout or yell it at the top of my voice. (I guess I was convinced that God had solved His "hearing problem.") I didn't even emphasize words. I just said, "Come, Holy Spirit." In a moment of time, He flooded that upper room with His Presence and engulfed the 100 people gathered there. They started to fall down, they started to laugh, and they started to weep. The joy of the Lord came in a wonderful, wonderful way that we had never experienced before.

Everyone enjoyed it so much that we all agreed to continue to meet together on Sunday night for quite awhile, and the people were so impressed with the change in me that they wanted to *make more room.* They wanted it to be more than just a Sunday night service. They literally said, "Let's make room for *more* to come." We had just stepped up to God's banqueting table with extra large platters. The first response of our enthusiastic congregation was to raise enough money to send Lois and I to Toronto, Ontario, so we could attend the renewal meetings at Toronto Airport Christian Fellowship. They were only throwing more fuel on the fire.

I've already described how Lois and I were first touched by God during our visit to Toronto, but there is more. In a meeting the morning after we received prayer, John Arnott told the people at the conference that Lois and I had come from Sunderland, England, the place where Smith Wigglesworth received the baptism of the Holy Spirit, and the birthplace of the Pentecostal movement in Europe. Then he invited me onstage and I told the people a little bit about the rich history of Sunderland as a center of revival. In particular, I described a plaque mounted outside of All Saints Parish Church that commemorates the revival of 1907. Then I told them that I wanted to take the fire of revival home with me to Sunderland, just as Alexander Boddy carried the revival fires home to Sunderland from the Welsh Revival ignited through the ministry of Evan Roberts. I longed to see the day when we would put up a plaque marking the arrival of revival in our day! At that point, John Arnott prophesied to me, "Ken, as surely as you stand beside me today, revival will come to Sunderland!"

Staggered by His Presence

As the week in Toronto progressed, we received prayer from Randy Clark, from numerous prayer intercessors, and from Guy Chevreau's wife, Janice. When she prayed for us at the end of the week, a spirit of joy engulfed us, and I was to learn that God was stripping away all the dignity I had so carefully crafted. It began the moment we decided to head for our car in the parking lot at Toronto. James and Lois were nearly to the car before they realized I was no longer with them. They came back and met me as I crawled on hands and knees across the lot toward the car. When we reached our hotel, the only way I could attain the safety of my bed was to crawl on my hands and knees across the parking lot, through the front doors, across the lobby, past the receptionist, and upstairs to the hotel room. So much for dignity.

When we finally made our way back to Sunderland, the entire church body was eagerly awaiting a full report on our trip. The church building was packed from wall to wall. (I suppose they just wanted to see where their investment had gone.) Everybody and their dog was there, and there was an incredible expectancy in the air. After a time of worship, I said, "James, will you come up here? Now James is going to share what happened to him in Toronto."

James came up to the pulpit, somewhat unsteadily, and gripped the Plexiglas like he was afraid he was going to fall. Then he started to cry, but managed to say, "I think if God lives anywhere on earth, then I think I've just been to His house. Wh-o-o-o." Then he fell on the floor, and that was it.

"Okay," I said, "now Lois is going to share."

That is when our keyboard player fell off of his stool in the orchestra pit we had in those days. All we could hear from the pit were groans and moans, and I said, "It's okay, it's okay, it's God." Then Lois came to give her testimony, but all she could do was cry. She just cried and cried without saying anything, and then she fell down too.

Then it was my turn, and my mind was filled with desperate prayers like, *God, these people have come to see a return on their investment. I've got to give them **something**. We can't just cry and fall down. After all, they paid tithes, for goodness' sake.* So I did everything in my power to stay on my feet. I gripped that pulpit so hard that my knuckles turned white, but I did manage to tell them something (although I can't remember what it was). Then I remember thinking, *Now we've got to pray for these people,* and I felt myself begin to lean backward for no logical reason. It got so bad that I had to hike my leg up in front of me just to counter balance this backward lean! Then I remember saying this, "If you want this…" (and "this" was that cockeyed leaning stance on one leg), "If you want this, then come and get it."

Do you know what happened next? Ninety-eight percent of the people stampeded down to the front! Suddenly we were surrounded by hundreds of hungry people. They just stood there looking at me, and I was thinking, *Oh God. Remember what they said in Toronto? You can only pray if you've received. Well, there's only the three of us, and two are on the floor.* (I knew that even if I counted Shawn, the keyboard man, in our number, I'd still be down to one man left standing.)

I decided to lift my fallen comrades off the floor, and then we started to pray for everyone who had come up. We prayed for people until 3 o'clock in the afternoon! The fire had fallen on Sunderland, England.

After the prayer time, our sanctuary looked like a battlefield with bodies strewn from one end of the room to the other. It was just wonderful. Then I said, "You know, God's here, isn't He? He might not stay forever, so why don't we come back tonight and have another service, even though it isn't scheduled?" So they all went home and came right back again at 6 o'clock for our second renewal service. I somehow felt that those Vineyard songs had something to do with the renewal fire, and I knew God had put His anointing on them. Since we didn't know any of them, we just sang along with the CD recordings. We said, "Here's the song, here are the words, just sing along." It was terrific.

After the service that night, we said, "Why don't we come back tomorrow? God is here, so let's come while He's here." And we did. Then we said, "Let's come back Tuesday." "Let's come back Wednesday." "Let's come back Thursday and Friday and Saturday." When we came around to Sunday morning again, we said, "Let's come back tonight!"

We went through the whole routine again the next week—Monday, Tuesday, Wednesday, Thursday, Friday, Saturday, and ended up at the end of the service on Sunday morning again, saying, "Let's come back...." By that time, we had been meeting together and experiencing the wonderful Presence of God for two weeks, and the word got out: "God has turned up at Sunderland Christian Centre!" Without advertising, promotion, phone campaigns, or gimmicks, the people started to come in from Baptist churches, Methodist churches, Anglican parishes, Plymouth Brethren and Presbyterian churches, and from Roman Catholic congregations. They all had one thing in common: They wanted *more* of God. As I watched this miracle unfold and saw the Body of Christ coming together right in front of my eyes, the Lord said, "Expand again, Ken. Enlarge again. I want to increase your capacity I want you to make a room, a dwelling place, for Me."

Suddenly we became a renewal center, and we knew it was yet another entrustment. Renewal and revival had come from the Lord to Sunderland to facilitate renewal for the whole of England and Europe. The world was welcome if they wanted to come, and come they did—from Australia, the Netherlands, Japan, Germany, France, and more. We became known as "Europe's Toronto," because we were a place where God was releasing His blessing.

I ask you today, have you made room for everything God wants to do through and in you? Have you made room? He is looking for expanding, flexible vessels that He can entrust with His treasures and dreams for the earth. Are you a vessel "meet for the Master's use"? (see 2 Tim. 2:21 KJV)

Endnote

1. James Strong, *Strong's Exhasutive Concordance of the Bible* (Peabody, MA: Hendrickson Publishers, n.d.), **persuaded** (Heb., #2388).

Chapter 2

The Call Is
Greater Than the Fall

For a righteous man may fall seven times and rise again…
(Proverbs 24:16).

When the phone rang, I had barely put the receiver to my ear when I heard these words: *"Brother, the call is greater than the fall!"* I instantly knew who it was. "Cleddie?"

Cleddie Keith is a pastor from Florence, Kentucky, who likes to deliver memorable, one-liner nuggets of wisdom to people the moment they pick up their phones. For that reason, he never has to identify himself (at least, not after his first surprise call). "Ken," Pastor Cleddie said, "Somebody on the Internet just told me, ' The call is greater than the fall.' *They are right!* If that isn't true, then God would never have come to Adam the very next day in the same way He came the day before!"

Now that got *me* going. God came at the same time and in the same way in the same place to the same man as He had before because the call on Adam's life was greater than his fall. God wouldn't have come to David through the prophet Nathan if the call on David's life was not greater than his fall! Jesus wouldn't have come to Peter on the beach if the call on Peter's life was not greater than his fall. My thoughts immediately landed on the entrustment God gave me in East Sunderland. Where have your thoughts landed?

We all experience "falls" in our lives. The term *fall* usually refers to moral failure. However, a better word would be *failure*. Every one of us has failed at some time. Most of our failures can be traced to disobedience of some kind. But some of us fall into moral sin, others experience financial failure, and still others fall victim to calamity or disease though we've done nothing to cause them. Sometimes we fail because of a direct assault of the devil on our lives or ministries, but most of the time we simply feel that we are failures as ministers, parents, or individuals struggling to follow God in a fallen world. I can guarantee you this much: The devil will show up to remind you of your fall.

You need to understand that *the devil can't talk to us about our call; he can only talk to us about our failures*. In fact, he'll talk, and talk, and talk about it; and then he'll talk about it some more. The devil wants you to be steeped in the failure of your fall, but God never talks to us about our fall. *God always talks to us about the call.* He is the God of mercy and grace who comes to us time and time again to lift us over our failures to reinforce the call upon our lives. Can I tell you this today? God is incredibly in love with your heart! He is more pleased with those things in your heart that He loves than displeased with those things that disappoint Him.

God had rewarded the Shunammite woman for her diligence in preparing a place and making room for His prophet in her house. Whenever you expand and stretch to make a prophetic bed for God's purposes, God will give you the secret desire of your heart. Elisha asked the Shunammite woman about the desire of her heart, and was puzzled about what he could do for her. Finally Gehazi mentioned that the woman had no son.

Then [Elisha] said, "About this time next year you shall embrace a son." And she said, "No, my lord. Man of God, do not lie to your maidservant!" But the woman conceived, and bore a son when the appointed time had come, of which Elisha had told her (2 Kings 4:16-17).

Go Back to the Promise

That son born by prophetic promise grew into a young man, and one day he went to meet his father who was working with some men harvesting a crop. Suddenly this young man collapsed and was carried home to his mother where he died. Suddenly her hope, her dream, her promise, was dead. The Shunammite woman never forgot where her son came from—he was the physical fruit of a prophetic promise. In her mind, there was only one place to go when her son of promise suddenly died before his time.

*And she went up and **laid him on the bed of the man of God**, shut the door upon him, and went out. Then she called to her husband, and said, "Please send me one of the young men and one of the donkeys, that I may **run to the man of God**..." (2 Kings 4:21-22).*

The Shunammite woman took her dead son—her dead dream and her dead promise—straight to the room that she had made for God's man and laid him on the prophetic bed! There are times when we are glad we've made a room for God. That room, that bed of accommodation for God's ways, becomes our place of refuge, a hiding place where we can go in times of trouble, testing, tribulation, and persecution. You will thank God for the prophetic bed you made long ago when everything concerning your promise, your dream, and your heart's desire suddenly seems to collapse and die in your lap.

One of the most serious problems with many Christians today is that they never go to the trouble or sacrifice to make room for God when everything is fine and things look good. Unfortunately, if we haven't made the room for God in the good times, then we will have no place to go when things go wrong in life. Nothing takes the place of making room for God when He visits us. Once things start to collapse, we often find that the church meetings and conferences can't help us, and neither can the stack of Christian books. In the day of trouble, there is nothing quite so miraculous and reassuring as the place in our heart that we have prepared for God.

When things get bad, you need to do what the Shunammite woman did. She took her dead son and laid him on the bed. What bed? The prophetic bed—the bed she had prepared for the move of God personified in the life of Elisha. Had she not been willing to have her life and home disrupted and reorganized, she would have had no place to take her dead son.

Sometimes God gives us the desire of our heart and yet, after we live with it for awhile, it just seems to die in our hands. Nearly every person I've ever met has had a dream that lived for awhile, and then died. Nearly everyone who has entered the full-time ministry knows what it is like to launch a local church ministry or evangelistic outreach under prophetic declaration through the power of God. Most will tell you that after the work thrived and grew for awhile, a time came when it seemed to wither away or die. What would you do if this happened to you? Consider what the Shunammite woman did. She laid her dead dream on the prophetic bed she had made, and then she *ran to the man of God*. Under the new covenant of Jesus Christ, we should run to God Himself.

> *...So it was, when the man of God **saw her afar off**, that he said to his servant Gehazi, **"Look, the Shunammite woman!** Please **run now to meet her**, and say to her, 'Is it well with you? Is it well with your husband? Is it well with the child?' " And she answered, "It is well" (2 Kings 4:25-26).*

I love the part in Second Kings 4 when Elisha's servant asks on behalf of the prophet, "Where's the boy?" This woman didn't tell the servant that her son was dead; she just said, "It is well." What she was really thinking was, *It will be well as soon as I get to the one who made the promise.*

The moment the Shunammite woman reached Elisha, she caught him by the feet and wouldn't let go (although Elisha's servant, Gehazi, was ready to push her away). This is where the relationship comes into play. Elisha knows this woman. They have a prophetic history together; they share the memory of the day Elisha prophetically declared that she would bear a son as a reward for making room and provision for God (see 2 Kings 4:16). Although the woman never mentioned the fact that this same son was now dead, the prophet knew something serious was wrong with her by her reference to a statement she made the day God made His promise to her (see 2 Kings 4:27-28).

Once the woman's painful sorrow was revealed, the prophet gave his staff—the outward symbol of his prophetic authority—to Gehazi, his servant, with orders to lay the staff on the deceased boy's face. Soon the servant returned with the news that his efforts with Elisha's staff had failed.

Believe God for a Resurrection

Everything that was done through a merely human intermediary didn't work. The prophetic bed in your life is something sacred. It is a memory and a sacred covenant process you share with God Himself. Elisha now faced a major challenge unlike any he had ever faced before. The boy he had prophesied into being was now dead. But as he looked around that room, he could point out every crack in the ceiling and describe every mark on the walls. He knew all about the bed where the dead son of promise rested in total silence. This prophet had spent hours in that room in the presence of Jehovah God. I can just imagine him saying, "God, You are the same God who spoke to me in this very room. As I rested on this same bed, You visited me in the night hours, and You came to me with miraculous answers to my prayers. O God, You know this room better than I know it! Come in Your power and do something with this boy."

I want the Holy Spirit to be familiar with my heart. Let me say that again: *I want the Holy Spirit to be familiar with my heart.* I don't want Him to feel like a stranger when His Presence is manifested in me. I want Him to say, "Yes, I'll come; I know this place. It was made just for Me. I'm familiar with it because I spend a lot of time here."

Elisha's answer to death perfectly symbolizes what the Holy Spirit does in our lives. That old prophet laid his body right on top of that dead boy! The Law of Moses didn't matter in that moment of crisis when death lay face to face with life. Like the Messiah who would come years later, the prophet was on a mission to breathe life where there was only death. The Law commanded every Israelite not to touch the dead or they would be unclean. This prophet must have reasoned, "Well, this dead boy isn't going to be dead for long!"

Elisha the prophet laid his own body on top of the corpse of this son of promise—eye to eye, mouth to mouth, and hand to hand. The Holy Ghost wants to lay Himself right on top of your dead dreams and fallen hopes, because He is determined to see a resurrection in your life! God is a prophetic God. Everything God does is prophetic. Every time God speaks, it's prophetic. Every promise He makes is prophetic. God the Holy Spirit wants to lie on your dream tonight. Take the heavenly vision that has died in your hands and place it in the prophetic bed you made for God in days gone by. Trust Him. He wants to lie on it in all of His glory—eye to eye, mouth to mouth, hand to hand.

God wants your eyes to see that vision once again. He wants to breathe the breath of life into it again. He wants you to feel its warmth and life once more. In the case of the Shunammite woman, God supernaturally restored life to her prophetic son of promise.

The same Spirit who raised Jesus Christ from the dead is alive in you (see Rom. 8:11). He is anointed to resurrect your dream, your vision, your goal, and your destiny—but first you need to return to the room you prepared for God before He gave you that vision, goal, and destiny. Return to the prophetic words you received and confirmed in your heart. Remember the faith that God planted in your heart to see it birthed into reality. Are you willing to abandon your dreams as lost and gone? Will you lay your dead or dying promise from God on the bed you made for His purposes, only to see it buried and left to disintegrate in failure? You don't have to. Lay it on that prophetic bed and run to the Presence of God. Wrap your arms of faith around the feet of God and say, "It is well." Are you willing to believe God for a resurrection?

Pray this prayer over your lost and lifeless dreams and visions:

I remember the promise You gave me. I still remember how it gripped my heart and how it was embedded in my spirit, but God, it seems like it's just died. I don't even know where it is anymore, but I'm willing for You to come and lie upon it again, to breathe life into it again. I've made room for You, Lord. There is still a bed reserved only for You in my heart. I've laid my fallen dream and lifeless promise on Your bed, Lord. Will You come again, as You've done so many, many times before? Come to the room I made for You, and come with purpose. I'm asking You to come—not just for fellowship, not just for a meal, not just to rest—but to raise back to life that which has died.

Whatever has died in your life—your marriage, your ministry, or another vision—*lift it up to Him*. It could be a prayer ministry, a ministry to the poor, a gang ministry, or youth work. No matter what it is, if God gave it to you and now it has died, the power of the Holy Spirit is here to resurrect it. The dream will live again. Ask the Holy Spirit to come and lie upon it, eye to eye, mouth to mouth, and hand to hand.

After Elisha lay on that boy, *he looked for the signs of recovery,* and the Bible says the child became warm. Look for the signs of recovery and resurrection in your fallen entrustment. If necessary, ask God to lie on your fallen dream a second time. Nothing is beyond the touch of God.

God Talks About Your Call

My heart just breaks everytime I read about the day Jesus met Peter and the disciples on the beach in John 21. I marvel at how gently and patiently Jesus worked with Peter, the man who denied and cursed Him when a young servant "accused" the rough fisherman of being with Jesus. It paints a wonderful picture of God's mercy and love toward "the called who have fallen."

I can almost hear Jesus say, "Peter, you haven't even lifted your head because you can't face Me. I understand. It is because the last time we faced one another like this, I was led away to die after you denied Me and fled away in shame and guilt. You thought you could never fix your eyes on Me again." Then I can hear Jesus say, "Peter, come here. Now lift your head and look—fix your gaze on Me again. Look at these eyes." It's wonderful, isn't it? This is a picture of what God did in my life too.

Peter only had thoughts of his fall, but this dialogue with the Master had little to do with Peter's fall. It was all about the call! Jesus put His arm around Peter's shoulder and walked him down the beach, but He didn't talk about Peter's fall. He was only interested in Peter's call. He said, "If you love Me, Peter, then feed My sheep. Feed My sheep," (see Jn. 21:15-17). Perhaps Jesus also reminded Peter about the time He said, "...you are Peter, and on this rock I will build My church, and the gates of Hades shall not prevail against it" (Mt. 16:18). Peter may have been impetuous and often put his foot in his mouth, but God loved the "yes" in him—the "yes" that caused Peter to get out of the boat and walk on water.

Friend, today I say to you again, God is incredibly in love with your heart. He is speaking to you about your call, not your fall. Resurrect your dreams and allow Him to breathe life into your hopes. You are chosen; you are His. He loves you!

Chapter 3

Pursue Your Entrustment

For we are God's fellow workers; you are God's field, you are God's building

(1 Corinthians 3:9).

Obviously God could get the job done all on His own. He doesn't *need* us; He *wants* us. He could speak in an audible voice and bring every man, woman, and child to their knees in an instant. He could send angels on any of our assignments and they would get them done quickly. God doesn't need us; He wants us. For some reason, He dares to put entrustments in our lives, even though we know we are generally less than dependable. He calls each of us for a purpose, saying, "This is what I've called you for. This is your entrustment."

Perhaps like many readers, you are tempted to skip any Scripture passages reproduced in books like this, but I urge you to reject that enticement this time and read the following quote from beginning to end. This brief passage from the Book of Isaiah has a lot to do with entrustments and enticements.

Is this not the fast that I have chosen: To loose the bonds of wickedness, to undo the heavy burdens, to let the oppressed go free, and that you break every yoke? Is it not to share your bread with the hungry, and that you bring to your house the poor who are cast out; when you see the naked, that you cover him, and not hide yourself from your own flesh? Then your light shall break forth like the morning, your healing shall spring forth speedily, and your righteousness shall go before you; the glory of the Lord shall be your rear guard. Then you shall call, and the Lord will answer; you shall cry, and He will say, "Here I am." If you take away the yoke from your midst, the pointing of the finger, and speaking wickedness, if you extend your soul to the hungry and satisfy the afflicted soul, then your light shall dawn in the darkness, and your darkness shall be as the noonday. The Lord will guide you continually, and satisfy your soul in drought, and strengthen your bones; you shall be like a watered garden, and like a spring of water, whose waters do not fail. Those from among you shall build the old waste places; you shall raise up the foundations of many generations; and you shall be called the Repairer of the Breach, the Restorer of Streets to Dwell In. If you turn away your foot from the Sabbath, from doing your pleasure on My holy day, and call the Sabbath a delight, the holy day of the Lord honorable, and shall honor Him, not doing your own ways, nor finding your own pleasure, nor speaking your own words, then you shall delight yourself in the Lord; and I will cause you to ride on the high hills of the earth, and feed you with the heritage of Jacob your father. The mouth of the Lord has spoken (Isaiah 58:6-14).

This passage from the Book of Isaiah has become a "life Scripture" to us in Sunderland, and in particular to Lois and I. We go to it often to remind ourselves why God has called us in the first place. We were led to establish a ministry called Revival Now to fulfill this scriptural mandate as a mercy missions ministry.

Honestly, this Scripture in Isaiah 58 is one of the last Scriptures I would ever want to go to in the Bible. It doesn't have the happy appeal of one of the many "blessing" Scriptures God has given us. Yet it is something He has given us to meditate upon and cherish. Even more to the point, this "chosen fast" passage is an entrustment that we have been assigned to fulfill in East Sunderland. I was reminded that Jesus said, "For you have the poor with you always..." (Mt. 26:11), and "...Assuredly, I say to you, inasmuch as you did it to one of the least of these My brethren, you did it to Me" (Mt. 25:40).

Lois and I have concluded that we are to pour out our lives to the poor. Cindy Jacobs prophesied that God was going to take us "to the darkest and the hardest countries of the world." I wish I could tell you we said, "Amen, we'll go!" with no hesitation, but the truth is that our flesh didn't really want to do it. Nevertheless, we did say "yes."

One of the sobering facts about God's entrustments is that it cost God everything to entrust things to us. We've already noted that God can get the job done all on His own, or through His angels. Yet He chose to call us His building, His field, and His "raw material" of choice. It was difficult for me to admit that God didn't really need Ken Gott, but that He had chosen to *want* me despite the real risk that I will fail. It was in this light that the Lord began to speak to me about an entrustment.

My Grandfather's Watch

For the sake of illustration, suppose my grandfather gave me a 24-carat antique gold pocket watch. This heirloom was hand-engraved and priceless to the family. Once it was handed down to me, I kept it and carefully preserved it for a number of years until I was assigned to lead a long-term missions outreach project that required me to spend many years overseas. I knew I had to commit the watch to someone else's care, so I decided to call a good friend. "Friend, do you remember that beautiful gold pocket watch my grandfather gave me?" "Yes, it's the hand-engraved watch with the nice chain." "Do you know that it still keeps beautiful time to this day?"

"Listen, I'm going to be involved in a long-term project overseas and I can't take this watch with me since I'll be on the go all the time. Since this is one of my family's most prized heirlooms, I can't leave it with just anyone. I'll have a grandson one day, and I'll want to pass it along to him. So I want to entrust this gold watch to you, because I trust you. If you agree to do it, then I want you to look after it like it was your own. Every now and then you'll need to take it out, polish it, and wind it up to maintain its working parts and preserve its value. If you should notice that it's not keeping time, then I want you to take it straight to a reputable watch-maker and get it repaired. Is this something you are willing to do for me? Good. The family will reward you generously for your assistance, I can assure you. My friend, I'm giving this heirloom to you as an entrustment. In about ten years' time, I'm going to come back and I'll ask you for this watch. Thank you."

Let's say I committed the watch into my friend's care, and life went on. Ten years later, I returned from abroad and found that my grandson, who was born shortly after I left, was mature enough to appreciate and care for his great, great grandfather's heirloom.

When I finally tracked down my friend in another city, I asked him, "Do you remember that gold pocket watch I entrusted to you ten years ago?" I won't be very happy if my friend blinks as if he doesn't know what I'm talking about, and then says, "Oh, yeah. I remember it now. I'm sure you realize that I've moved to different houses and cities at least two or three times since then. But don't worry—I'm sure it's in a box in the garage. I think it's there."

I would consider this friend's language and casual attitude to be alarming at best. Why? Because I gave him a treasured entrustment of great value, and *it cost me something* to do that. I risked the potential loss or damage to an irreplaceable heirloom because I trusted this friend. If after ten years, I discover that he dumped my grandfather's precious gold watch into a box like a used battery or a long-forgotten childhood rock collection, then I wouldn't be very happy about things. My heart would sink if I had to listen to him rummaging through boxes and drawers in his damp basement while I waited. It wouldn't do him much good to say, "Don't worry," if he is unable to find the watch while I am there. Nor would it do to call me two days later and cheerfully say, "Hey, Ken, I found it." I would regret my entrustment if, when he finally puts the watch in my hand, I notice that it is badly tarnished. That would tell me my friend never bothered to polish it once he "filed it" in the box of forgetfulness. Worse yet, how would I feel if the mechanisms on the inside were hopelessly frozen and irreparable? I would be upset if this friend failed to keep my family heirloom in working order, or if I discovered that what he gave me simply was not the same watch I gave him ten years ago (thanks to neglect and carelessness). This friend failed to handle the entrustment.

God prepared me from birth to receive an entrustment, but it wasn't always so obvious. I remember the days when nobody cared whether God showed up or not—we acted like we could have church without Him. Like everyone else, I came to church out of duty rather than desire. The routine was simple: You pay your tithes, you listen to the sermon, and then you file out of the church building in exactly the same condition as when you came in (only hungrier). There was no desire or spiritual hunger, and consequently God didn't show up. My childhood memories of church life are filled with stale religious images of everyone going through the motions. (Yes, even us Pentecostals. We just had "motions" some of the older churches didn't have or approve of.) This kind of church atmosphere was all I knew well into my early teens.

Then at the age of 17, God impacted my life. This had more to do with my own desire for Him than with any particularly spectacular event in the church. I was baptized in the Holy Spirit, and then I met and married Lois in 1976. I was called into the ministry in 1983 while still serving as a "Bobby," or English policeman. After working in my father-in-law's church as home group leaders, Lois and I borrowed some people from our home group and started a work in Sunderland as an official outreach from the church in August of 1985.

A History of the Gotts' Entrustment

For about four years, we met in a historic YMCA building in Sunderland. This building had hosted the likes of D.L. Moody, Ira Sankey, and Stephen Jeffries in the previous century—all of whom held powerful evangelistic campaigns there. We didn't know it at first, but we were literally beginning to dig out the old wells of anointing first dug by the fiery pioneers of Christ who went before us.

After four years had passed, I felt the Lord was leading us to a one-acre plot of land in East Sunderland. It wasn't much to speak of because it was just a bit of waste ground right in the middle of a slum area. Apartment buildings stood just across the road from the location, offering a very forgettable view. If they weren't there, however, you would only have seen more squalor and disintegration behind them. These government-sponsored apartment complexes weren't what you would call "nice" apartment buildings. They were home to virtually every social problem and criminal enterprise you have ever heard about on the news or imagined in your mind—and more. Fully 25 percent of all the crimes committed in Sunderland (a city of 300,000) were committed in our neighborhood, and one in three juvenile crimes were committed right around our church site. Yet God led us divinely to that plot of land and said, "I want you to put up a community church here for this community." We had just been given a divine entrustment planted in the heart of Sunderland's worst area—a place plagued by high crime, impossible social problems, and no spiritual witness whatsoever. We had been commissioned to take hope into a hole of despair.

From our very first meeting in the YMCA basement to this day, we have enjoyed phenomenal success in our meetings. We began with a dedicated core of determined believers (whom we call "the Dales Six" because they were part of our small home group). They embraced the vision as their own and continually sacrificed their comfort, time, and finances to see it come to pass. We watched as God performed miracle after miracle to help us plant a work in East Sunderland.

In 1991, God helped us build a church costing approximately $880,000 (U.S. dollars) with a congregation of only 120 people (if you included the children). It was built with sacrificial giving and no gimmicks or professional fund-raisers. The people responded to the spirit of giving that God sent to the church. Many people sold houses and gave their equity to build the vision. In response to an elder's prophetic word, I challenged every family that felt called of God to give £10,000 (or about $16,670). Surprisingly enough, people went back and took that word to heart and started to donate large amounts of money to the dream. I remember brides actually canceling their weddings so they could donate their savings to the building fund! It was just a phenomenal time of giving, and we built a church building on a one-acre plot of land right in the middle of a crime center near the docks in East Sunderland.

Even the acquisition of the land required a miracle. Land is hard to come by on a small island inhabited by millions of people, so when city planners have to choose between giving land to a corporation or a church congregation, the church people almost always lose out. God had different plans this time. When one of our care group leaders held a barbecue in his back garden (backyard), he invited the family next door over and asked me to deliver a short message. The entire family came to Christ that day. It so happened that the head of this family heard about our desire to build and asked me about it. He was a "quantity surveyor" for the local zoning and land authority, and he assured me that we could get what we needed—no matter how many times we had been turned down already. He returned a few days later to offer me my choice of three different land sites, and then guided us through the whole building process. God had once again miraculously supplied a key man to bring His vision to pass. We celebrated our grand opening in March of 1992.

However, it wasn't until 1995, after one year of nightly renewal services, that the Lord began to speak clearly about His entrustment to me. He seemed to be saying, "Ken, do you love Me? Then give this building to this community. Give it away." At first I wanted to argue on behalf of the people who had given sacrificially to build that building, but He reassured me that He would take care of the details if I would only step out and obey by faith. I gave it to God and then shared the word with the elders of the church. I was shocked to discover that they were in total agreement, and the congregation felt the same way! We began by opening up our church building to more and more outreach efforts while praying about a new home for the main congregation. It was exciting, exhausting, and stretching, to say the least.

Crown House Miracle

However, God immediately came through when two local businessmen dropped the keys to Crown House into my hand on June 5, 1996, a ten-story building that offered ten times what I had given away. But I knew there were some very large and overwhelming challenges attached to receiving a ten-story building that had been vacant for four years. For one thing, I was told it would cost about £30,000 ($50,000 U.S. dollars) to turn on the electricity and heat and to get the elevators (or lifts, as we call them in England) in operating order.

When John and Carol Arnott visited Sunderland and ministered at the church, we took them on a tour of the vacant building God had just given us. I told John, "You know this building isn't for me; it is for the Body of Christ. The Lord just told me to facilitate this thing, so I'm going to move in here as a tenant and pay rent just like anybody else. I'm not going to own this building; I'm just going to facilitate it."

During the tour of Crown House, the power of God came over Carol Arnott, and she saw sparks coming out of the

Crown House building that fired across the North Sea and landed in the red-light district of Amsterdam. As they hit the windmills, they were propelled into mainland Europe, including France, a nation that has never seen a true revival in its existence. Less than five percent of the population in France is Christian. Carol also saw the sparks showering the nations in the former eastern bloc of the Soviet Union, including Albania, Romania, Bulgaria, Hungary, Czechoslovakia, Bosnia, and others.

John asked me how much it would cost to get the place running and I gave him the £30,000 figure. John looked at the building and said, "Ken, I think you'll need a hundred thousand pounds" ($167,000). I shook my head and said, "I don't think so," but he answered, "We'll look for it anyway." John received an offering for the Crown House project in our renewal service that night and £50,000 (about $83,350) came in! Later on, an Australian prophet, Steve Penny, and Kathy Lechner from Florida felt led to take up an offering for Crown House at our prophetic conference, and the same amount was given to help us reach Europe with the gospel.

John Arnott was right. We spent a full £100,000 and more just to bring Crown House up to building safety code standards. We were discovering that God's provision was abundant and timely in every detail.

For instance, how do you furnish a massive ten-story office building like Crown House? I wanted ministries to come in and I didn't want to charge them anything, but it was no small challenge to find furniture, carpet, flooring, and all the necessary items needed to outfit a place like Crown House! The first thing Lois and I did was to establish a limited or non-profit organization to handle the managerial and financial aspects of Crown House. All the rent monies and payment disbursements would go through that organization instead of through Lois and I. This allowed us to obey God's command that we *steward* instead of *own* the Crown House entrustment.

I knew that God had given us a mandate to bring in anointed ministries from around the world who shared our vision to reach Europe for Christ. We wanted each of these ministries to have an office overlooking the North Sea to serve as an European ministry base so they wouldn't have to worry about carpet, furniture, phone systems, or high office rental fees. When we gave our church building to the community by faith and began remodeling Crown House, God opened Heaven's floodgates of provision again.

We didn't know it, but God was working another miracle through a quiet Christian gentleman named George Cooke. George founded and managed a non-profit charity in London that helps other charities. He lives in a modest house on a modest income, but his accomplishments are anything but modest. When George learned that one of Britain's largest companies, based in the largest building in London, was downsizing their London operation, he made an appointment with the top officer of the corporation.

After the usual greetings, George asked this man, "What are you going to do with all this furniture and the carpets after you complete the downsizing process?" The man said, "We are going to sell off most of it, and we will donate a little bit of it too." George said, "You've got a problem." That caught the officer's attention. "What do you mean?"

George said, "Let's say you donate a chair to a charity worker who takes it back to his office. He sits down on it, falls back, and breaks his neck. He would sue you for two million pounds." "Why is that?" the company officer asked. "Well, it's because he knows you are a large company and can afford it." The officer nodded and shook his head. "Oh yeah."

"I can help you with that," George said. "How can you help us?" the man asked. "Let me handle the liquidation process through my charity," George said. "Give me sole distribution of all the furniture and the carpet. I'll take care of it for you, and I'll give you a little retainer for it as well. That way, if anything happens, it comes back on me and not on you. We don't have any money, so no one will sue us. We're a charity." The executive quickly said, "That's great. That's brilliant," and they signed the deal, giving George total distribution rights to all the firm's expensive Italian and Scandinavian furniture and workstations, and pallets of carpet tiles that were so new you could still smell the newness on them.

As soon as George Cooke signed the papers with the firm, *his next trip was to Sunderland to see me*. A friend and former business manager of mine took George on a tour of Crown House and he told me, "Ken, you've got to meet this guy. I think he might help us." That is how George Cooke ended up having supper with me that evening.

George is a very proper Londoner who speaks flawless "Queen's English" like the best BBC (British Broadcasting Corporation) announcer—that is, until the Spirit of God hits him. So George was sitting opposite from me in a restaurant when he looked at me and in his usual non-expressive way, said, "Ken, I've been through Crown House. I could actually furnish every office in that building and put carpets down anywhere you wanted them—in all ten floors—for nothing. Would you like that?"

I wanted to shout, "*Y-e-e-e-s-s-s!*" I wanted to run up the ceiling and down the walls! It took everything within me just to contain myself, but I found myself saying in my most controlled and nonchalant tone, "George, that would be very nice." (I still can't believe it.)

Within three weeks, George Cooke kept his word and sent five full tractor-trailer loads of beautiful Italian and Scandinavian office furniture and workstations plus huge pallets of carpet tiles to the loading docks at Crown House! All of them were like new! We had so many carpet tiles that we've even decided to install them in the elevators (lifts) and the bathrooms. It is amazing that we got it all for nothing. The building was given to us, the furniture and carpet tiles were given to us, and the money to start the whole thing and remodel the first floor for our new church meeting facility in Crown House was given to us. Why? I believe it is because I obeyed God and gave a building to the poor. There is nothing that unites you more with the heart of God than extravagant giving to the poor.

A New Entrustment

I challenged everyone in the church who had a strong flow of mercy in their lives to stay with Hope House Community Church, and 100 people stayed to form the nucleus of the new church body located in the former Sunderland Christian Centre building. Situated only 200 yards away from Crown House, the mission of this church is to minister the gospel to the local community through innovative outreach programs and through practical, hands-on mercy ministries such as food and clothing ministries. The pastor of Hope House Community Church is a streetwise and compassionate man who knows the neighborhood and can identify with the people there.

The remaining church members moved up the street to the Crown House tower where City Church will pursue God's entrustment to be a regional "resource" church influencing greater Sunderland, the nation, and Europe. The two church bodies live and work together in total harmony because their visions and ministry focuses are completely different.

The pastor of Hope House focuses his evangelism efforts in the highly concentrated population within a half-mile radius of the church. He does not have conferences or large meetings, because that is my job. He is actively working to convert the church into a true cell church that is totally adapted to the specialized needs of the local community. Many people in inner city settings don't consider themselves "meeting goers." Their lifestyles, transportation limitations, and tougher living environment make intimate home groups or support meetings much more suitable for their needs.

As soon as we made these changes as an act of obedience, our ministries seemed to explode with new growth and effectiveness. At this writing, the Lord has entrusted me with the regional responsibility of supplying apostolic oversight for seven churches associated with Revival Now (our ministry organization) in the greater Sunderland area. As a part of our international entrustment, we are working directly with ministries from around the world who have been led supernaturally to join us as tenants and co-workers for European revival at Crown House. Each of these ministries has a strong call from the Lord to cooperate in a united effort to bring revival to Europe, exactly as the Lord told me they would.

I have discovered that when you join your heart with the heart of God for the poor, you hit a slipstream of favor and anointing that just keeps accelerating in speed and depth. Lois and I are deep in this slipstream of God's favor. Every day, something new from God's hand seems to bubble up or make its way into our lives.

What Is Your Entrustment?

Jesus Christ knew that He had an entrustment from His Father in Heaven. He came to live a sinless life as an ordinary man. He came to lay down His life on the cross and to die for our sins—even though we didn't deserve it. That was His entrustment, and He refused to be turned aside, enticed, or deterred from fulfilling His divine entrustment. People wanted to make Him king in place of Caesar. The devil wanted Him to bow before him in return for all earthly power. His mother and brothers seemed to want Him to stop being so controversial, and none of His disciples wanted Him to die on the cross. He pursued His entrustment with single-minded devotion, and He did it as a man, even though He was God. He drew the strength He needed the same way we are to do it—He pulled away from everything and everyone else. He spent entire nights in prayer on a remote mountain just to be with His Father. Like Jesus, you need to focus on the entrustment that your heavenly Father has given you.

Paul the apostle pleased God by properly handling his divine entrustment too. This rogue rabbi, this rebel with a cause, was changed in a moment of time and given a divine mandate, a heavenly entrustment, to defy Jewish conviction and law to bring the gospel of Jesus Christ to the Gentile world. How do we know he fulfilled his entrustment? At the end of his life, Paul described his entrustment to King Agrippa and how he handled it:

> *So I said, "Who are You, Lord?" And He said, "I am Jesus, whom you are persecuting. But rise and stand on your feet; for I have appeared to you for this purpose, to make you a minister and a witness both of the things which you have seen and of the things which I will yet reveal to you. I will deliver you from the Jewish people, as well as from the Gentiles, to whom I now send you, to open their eyes, in order to turn them from darkness to light, and from the power of Satan to God, that they may receive forgiveness of sins and an inheritance among those who are sanctified by faith in Me." Therefore, King Agrippa, I was not disobedient to the heavenly vision (Acts 26:15-19).*

Paul was saying, "King Agrippa, I handled the entrustment and resisted the enticements that the devil brought." Examine the lives of great saints. Notice what happened when they managed to keep themselves focused. Look at the life of Billy Graham. If ever there was a man who handled an entrustment, it is Billy Graham. I am sure that he was enticed or tempted to do a lot of other things—to be a statesman or a politician—but he resisted the enticements and kept handling the entrustment. As a result, he became one of this world's greatest evangelists with millions of souls marked to his account. Look at all the saints who risked their lives to pass the hope of the gospel to us through the Scriptures. They faithfully handled God's entrustment and we are the fruit of their labors.

When you faithfully handle an entrustment, God tends to bless you with even more entrustments and the favor and grace you need to handle them. We are constantly being approached by government officials, church leaders, and civic leaders who want to *give us* things like buildings, land, and entire church congregations because they trust us. Our city council has given us large auditoriums at almost no cost because they thought we could serve the needs of the community better through our ministry than they could through government programs alone. Church groups who are suffering from burnout have given us church buildings and the responsibility of ministering to and leading the congregations in those buildings. It isn't because of us; it is because of God and His grace.

Can God trust you? Is He able to look at your heart and say, "I can trust this one. I can trust this heart with My treasure"? The Lord wants to entrust His precious vision for the earth with you. He wants to entrust you with the *answers* to the prayers and needs of others. You are His fellow worker. You are His field and His building. He wants you to handle and take personal responsibility for a divine entrustment. It is up to you to run with it and properly handle it.

Our supreme model for life, Jesus Christ, knelt in the garden of Gethsemane and prayed to His Father, "I have glorified You on the earth. I have finished the work which You have given Me to do" (Jn. 17:4). The entrustment from the Father to the Son was, "Son, go to the earth and glorify Me." Jesus began His work by humbling Himself, by stripping away His rightful power and authority to enter the earth as a babe through the womb of a virgin. Thirty-three years later the Son looked to the Father and said, "Father, I have glorified You on the earth. I've handled the entrustment. I've finished the work."

How would you like to finish the work and complete your course before finishing your life? My father-in-law,

Herbert Harrison, served the Lord as a minister in the Assemblies of God of England for 48 years before he went to be with the Lord at the age of 75 while I was working on this book. He was suffering from a terminal disease in the last few months of his life, but I will never forget the day he said, "I'm at peace with myself, I'm at peace with the world, and I'm at peace with God. I've finished the course. I've done all that He's asked me to do." Oh, that all of us will be able to say what dear Herbert said at the end of his course in life. "I was faithful to the heavenly vision. I handled the entrustment."

I am still deeply involved in learning how to handle entrustments. I don't presume to tell you that I'm some kind of expert, and I don't suppose that I ever will become one. This book was birthed as much through my failures as through my successes. But I want to encourage you to run with everything that God has given you. If the Spirit of the Lord is speaking strongly to you about an entrustment you've been given and perhaps mishandled up to this point, then I should remind you that judgment begins with the house of God (see 1 Pet. 4:17). Has the Lord given you an entrustment that has somehow landed in a neglected corner of the basement of your life? Is your heart crying out, "Lord, I want to properly handle Your entrustments. I want to be able to honestly say, 'I've run the good race, I've completed my course.' "

If you are a minister entrusted with the equipping and discipling of others, you can begin to handle your entrustment by gathering good people around you and giving them opportunities to shine for Christ. You need to let the young men and women shine. Polish them. Cause them to sparkle, and let them be jewels in your crown. All you have to do is to handle the entrustment of God in God's way.

One of the biggest divine entrustments God has given to us all is *the use of His name*. We represent God and His Kingdom to other people around us by the way we live, serve, and obey Him. Even our pursuit of God's divine entrustment for our lives will directly affect the way our community, our government officials, and the lost view our God. Our goal should be to honestly say, like Jesus Christ before us, "Father, I have glorified Your name. I was faithful to the heavenly vision. I handled the entrustment. It is finished."

Chapter 4

Avoid Every Enticement

As I have said, thousands of people were streaming into our church from all over Europe and beyond. The Presence of God was so thick in our meetings that at times people could barely stand up. Rumors of God's move in our part of England had spread around the world to America, Japan, Australia, and Asia. We were being called "the Toronto of England," yet God spoke to me right in the middle of it all and told me that *I had failed....*

How could it be? Wasn't the whole world hungry for revival? Why would so many people make so many sacrifices to attend services in our church if what we were doing was so wrong? The problem wasn't revival or the lack of it, and it wasn't our hunger for more of God—we really did want more. The problem had to do with *obedience*. I had been enticed into disobedience and had forsaken my God-given entrustment—and I wasn't the first. King Saul is one of history's greatest "successful failures." He was good-looking, loved by the people, and a seemingly fearless leader who defeated his enemies in dramatic battles. He brought home entire herds of captured animals taken from fallen foes for sacrifice before Jehovah, and he led parades to celebrate the thousands of enemy soldiers he had killed. Yet God rejected him. Why? Samuel the prophet put it this way to King Saul:

> *...Has the Lord as great delight in burnt offerings and sacrifices, as in obeying the voice of the Lord? Behold, to obey is better than sacrifice, and to heed than the fat of rams. For rebellion is as the sin of witchcraft, and stubbornness is as iniquity and idolatry. Because you have rejected the word of the Lord, He also has rejected you from being king (1 Samuel 15:22-23).*

What I am about to share with you was received at great cost to my ego, but it could mean the difference between success and failure *in your life and ministry*. I am thankful to God that He arrested me and returned me to the path of obedience before it cost me something much more dear and difficult to replace.

With Entrustments Come Enticements

I've discovered the hard way that with every divine entrustment comes a set of enticements. When God trusts us with something precious from His heart, there is one way to succeed and many ways to fail. The key to God's favor is summed up in one word: *obedience.* Things can get confusing when we disobey because of good things, and they really get confused when we disobey because of godly things! In Saul's case, God had ordained that the sins of men be atoned for through the sacrifice of animals. But Saul failed to understand that what God really wanted was the true worship and praise provided by acts of obedience. His disobedience was an insult to God, an insult that Saul tried to cover up with a bribe of animal sacrifices. Although Saul seemed to be fearless on the battlefield, the fact is that he feared the disapproval of man more than the disapproval of God. He was a leader who failed to lead because he was a people-pleaser instead of a God-pleaser.

As we have outlined in the previous chapter, God told Lois and I to build a community church in East Sunderland's worst crime center near Sunderland's docks. We tackled the job with enthusiasm in the beginning and enjoyed a measure of instant success, but I began to steer the focus of the outreach in a different direction from God's original entrustment. Looking back upon that time, I must admit that when I came to Sunderland, I somehow felt like Sunderland was "waiting for me." I acted like there was now some hope for the city just because I showed up. I almost cringe when I see that my heart motives were as crude and misguided as that. Since my heart was wrong, it affected and tainted the way I looked at people. Instead of looking at people primarily out of relationship (although we were very strong in relationship), I looked at people and valued them by how they could be used to help me achieve what I wanted to achieve.

I must add here that heart relationships and a lifestyle of love have always been my wife's life flow. Because of this, we had an incredibly loving and united church. But the old leadership axiom, "As the leaders are, so the people are," is more true than we want to admit. I'm afraid that I passed along my performance-centered, approval-seeking compulsions to my people with unfortunate efficiency. Appearance and performance were everything. My worship band had to be really dressed up before I would even let them play a note on their instruments or sing in front of other people. The men had to wear dress shirts and ties, and the ladies had to wear nice dresses. As for me, I wasn't comfortable unless I made my entrance in a dark suit with a pressed white shirt and a tie. Everything had to be just right.

I would say things like, "God likes it this way. It impresses the Lord. The Holy Spirit likes to come into this environment." The problem was that once the public worship services were over and I found myself in a conversation with the Lord, my confident statements took on a hollow sound. I'd say, "Lord, I bet this impresses You...." The truth is that all our outward pomp and circumstance actually impresses Him very little. To a degree, it is necessary to devote some care to our outward appearance and behavior, *but God will always look first at our hearts.*

Obedience, Not Performance

I really felt uncomfortable when God began to respond to my grand statements about impressing Him. He said, "You know, I'll tell you what I'm about: I created the universe...." That is when my balloon deflated and I humbly told the Lord, "Well, You know, Lord, that *really is* impressive." Every time He caught me alone and away from my audience, He began to correct the error in my heart by comparing my puny accomplishments with His incomparable glory and majesty. That is when I began to realize just how much God really was impressed with my deeds and accomplishments—they were really nothing at all. He was after obedience, not performance.

When the move of God came to Sunderland, people began to stream in from other countries, as well as from cities throughout the British Isles. We had to make dramatic adjustments and go to nightly services to accommodate the crowds and security demands of the renewal. It was there, right in the midst of dramatic renewal and revival meetings, that the Spirit of God began to confront me with the stark reality that I was not handling my entrustments at all. I was pursuing enticements and building *my* kind of church—a high profile, huge, impressive regional church—when all the time God wanted a community church. We were trying to build upon a base of people drawn from suburban areas up to 20 miles (32 km) away. The Lord pulled me up short when He asked me, *"Ken, how many people from the local community come into your church?"*

Now let me paint a picture of this church building for just a moment. We had built a very nice $880,000 building right in the middle of Sunderland's poorest community. Then we surrounded it with an eight-foot security fence featuring large entrance gates for controlled entry and exit from the premises. The building had to have glass replaced with Plexiglas panels after continual breakages, and there were metal security shutters positioned over every entrance and exit. These shutters were rolled down and locked into place whenever the doors were not in active use and attended by security personnel.

God had called us to build a church for the needy and the poor in the East End of Sunderland, but our people had literally developed a siege mentality to wall themselves in *from* the community. They had to run in from their vehicles, and then we would close the doors and secure the entrances so we could "have church." We paid a security firm to watch our vehicles and protect the people coming to the services. This was necessary because auto theft and gang activity were constant threats. As a result, no one wanted to be the last one out of the building once our security service had left the premises.

One time our keyboard player left the building with his mother-in-law long after everyone else had gone—including the security personnel. When the two came out of the church building, they were suddenly attacked by gang members armed with stones and sticks. They managed to make it to their vehicle, but the gang members jumped up and down on their car, and some of the attackers were literally hanging onto the car doors as the two people frantically drove away! This should give you a general picture of the kind of environment found around the church building.

"Why would God put you there in the first place, Ken?" I believe that one reason God sent me there was specifically because it was contrary to my nature and what I believed was my call. I was still trying to avoid the difficult passage in Isaiah 58 at that time. I didn't realize it at first, but God was out to renew a whole lot more than just the local church body. He was starting at the "top" of the local leaders. He was out to reform and revive me in more ways than I was prepared to admit.

The first thing to happen when the renewal came with God's wonderful Presence, was that all my skewed performance values just seemed to disappear overnight. They were useless and meaningless in His Presence. That was when the Lord came to me and asked me the soul-piercing question: "Ken, when you stand before Me on that great and last day, when all the books are opened and nothing more can be written down, what do you think I'm going to ask you about?"

I wasn't sure what God wanted to ask me about, but I realized straight away what He would not ask me about. I knew He wouldn't be the least bit interested in my mailing list. I knew He wouldn't ask me about my tape sales or the number of people going to our meetings either. He wasn't a bit interested in hearing about how well we presented ourselves or how popular I had become with the people and with visiting church leaders. There would be no questions about how much I had achieved or how many times I had been asked to minister in other countries. I knew everything that God *wouldn't ask me about*, and the most disturbing thing about them was the fact that they were the only things that seemed important to me at the time. I began to realize there are certain things that God gives us that are unique to us—they are *entrustments*.

A Change in Perspective

I was experiencing an embarrassing and eye-opening "Joshua moment," and I'm not talking about God's dramatic charge to Joshua that he "be of good courage." Joshua also experienced a heart-changing encounter that "put him in his place" and changed the way he viewed God and His assignments.

> *And it came to pass, when Joshua was by Jericho, that he lifted his eyes and looked, and behold, a Man stood opposite him with His sword drawn in His hand. And Joshua went to Him and said to Him, "Are You for us or for our adversaries?" So He said, "No, but as Commander of the army of the Lord I have now come." And Joshua fell on his face to the earth and worshiped, and said to Him, "What does my Lord say to His servant?" Then the Commander of the Lord's army said to Joshua, "Take your sandal off your foot, for the place where you stand is holy." And Joshua did so (Joshua 5:13-15).*

I had made the same mistake that Joshua made. I had wrongly assumed and reasoned that since I had enjoyed God's blessings in my ministry, then He was so pleased that He had showed up to bless me and support my efforts. I was mistaken. God didn't show up to bless me, nor did He come to fight for me. If you ever find yourself asking the Lord, "Well, what about the church across the road, Lord? Are You for *them*, or are You for *us*?" then don't be surprised if you hear God say, "*Neither. I'm for Me.*"

God knew that I had a very important lesson to learn. He told me, "I don't need you; I want you. But if you don't handle this entrustment to the needy of this city, then I'll give it to someone who will." God came to ask me about His family treasure in Sunderland, and I was rummaging around in the junk box of my own ambitions and selfishness where I had carelessly lost it. I was learning that God doesn't want sacrificial service, gifts, or performance—He wants obedience.

Jesus is merciful, but He made it clear to His disciples that He isn't exactly delighted when we squander or mishandle the things He gives us. In His parable about the Kingdom of Heaven, Jesus showed how the steward who failed to properly handle his master's money had an excuse ready to justify his poor stewardship, but it didn't work:

> *Then he who had received the one talent came and said, "Lord, I knew you to be a hard man, reaping where you have not sown, and gathering where you have not scattered seed. And I was afraid, and went and hid your talent in the ground. Look, there you have what is yours." But his lord answered and said to him, "You wicked and lazy servant, you knew that I reap where I have not sown, and gather where I have not scattered seed. So you ought to have deposited my money with the bankers, and at my coming I would have received back my own with interest. Therefore take the talent from him, and give it to him who has ten talents. For to everyone who has, more will be given, and he will have abundance; but from him who does not have,*

even what he has will be taken away. And cast the unprofitable servant into the outer darkness. There will be weeping and gnashing of teeth" (Matthew 25:24-30).

This parable has been a favorite text for preachers and Christian leaders around the world, but I'm thinking that we all need to measure our own lives by this parable from time to time. I know things didn't go so well for me when I measured my ministry by this standard and found that I fell short of the mark. I'm learning that God is primarily concerned with being obeyed and seeing the knowledge of His glory cover the earth. It is time for us all to get in step with God instead of waiting for Him to match step with our little plans.

I have learned the hard way that whenever I pursue enticements—regardless of how godly and good they appear to be—then I will almost certainly fail to handle God's entrustments in my life. Too much of the time, we are being enticed by our egos and carried far from the heart of God by our own personal dreams and ambitions. We are so busy running after enticements that we forget all about our divine entrustment. My ministry work at Sunderland had been tainted by my wrong motives. Did I love God? Absolutely. Was I doing good things that seemed to honor God? Yes. Were people being blessed by God in our services and ministry? Yes. What was the problem then? I was so busy with good things that I had neglected my first call and entrustment to the people in the East End of our city. The Lord corrected me and put me back on the straight and narrow in His great love.

Wrong Motives, Wrong Methods

As I mentioned earlier, I was very driven and performance-oriented. I used to carefully study the ministry styles and methodologies of successful (or at least prominent) North American preachers, and I freely modeled my ministry and methods on the work of others. My motives were a mixture of a genuine desire to serve God and the hidden desire to look good. I wanted to be "anointed," and I reasoned that I could be anointed by copying anointed people. I didn't want to simply build a church in East Sunderland; I wanted to have the biggest church in the city. No, I wanted to have the biggest church in the Assemblies of God of England. There was only one problem with all that— God didn't give me that entrustment or assignment. My ambition and personal desires had become enticements to disobey and therefore to sin.

So God challenged me and exposed my enticements. Then He said, "Ken, I'll give you one more chance to put that community church in there." I am thrilled to tell you that God loves us so much that He has become the God of the second, third, fourth, fifth, sixth, and seventh chance for us! I can tell you from personal experience that when we fail God, He will come to us time after time with a gentle rebuke and yet another opportunity to repent and get it right. That's the grace and the mercy of the Lord.

In our case, God gave us a second chance by challenging us to essentially lose everything we had and step out on faith (which we will discuss in detail in later chapters). We thought our lives had been exciting up to that point, but the excitement had only begun! Lois and I discovered that when we began to properly handle God's entrustments, then He is free to abundantly bless us with miraculous provision and lasting fruit in our ministry and service. Obedience seems to be the key that helps us transcend earthly obstacles. It transports us supernaturally into God's stream of blessing, favor, and power.

Despite my enticement by success, God came to me and said, "You are still My building. You are still My field." You and I need to willingly jettison the weight of all the stuff that God never told us to keep or grasp for so that He can help us. If we will learn just to handle the entrustments He gives us and discard and disregard every enticement, then our obedience will take us to God's stream of anointing and destiny. When we do that, there is no doubt about our destination and the outcome of our mission.

This problem of entrustments and enticements is pervasive. By that I mean that we run into it on every level of our lives and ministries. You may find yourself delivering a prophecy to a small home group or a large conference, and you may sense a very strong anointing as you deliver the word. Things are going so well and the people are so receptive to your prophecy that when the Holy Spirit stops, you just have to keep on going. That is an enticement to go beyond an entrustment. If you are asked to pray for people in a prayer line, and God is speaking powerfully to one person after another through you, what do you do when the Spirit is clearly silent when you come to certain people in the line? If you simply pray a prayer of blessing (without passing it off as a prophecy or word of knowledge), then you have remained within the bounds of your entrustment. If you give in to the temptation to prophesy over these people as you did over others before them, then you have left your entrustment to trifle with an enticement.

If you are gifted in the area of the ministry of helps, but have always longed for the recognition and honor supposedly given to pulpit ministers, then you will almost certainly face enticements in the days ahead. Will you faithfully pursue your entrustment and find joy in God's call on your life, or will you actively search for every opportunity to preach or minister from behind a pulpit? Your answer and actions will mean the difference between an entrustment and an enticement. It all goes back to our image of God. If He is truly at work in us "both to will and to do" His perfect will (Phil. 2:13), then He is well able to move us into the ministry of His choice and design. If He doesn't call us to a thing, then we have no business seeking for it.

It's Never Too Late to Obey

Lois and I still face major enticements to veer from our entrustments, and in most cases, these enticements do not involve evil sins or evil people. On the contrary, many enticements involve godly duties and opportunities proposed and offered by godly people. What is an entrustment to the right person may be an enticement when offered to the wrong person. Most people don't realize that England, like the United States, divides itself roughly into north and south. The churches in the southern half of England tend to be well organized and enjoy recognized apostolic leadership by anointed people like Gerald Coates, Terry Virgo, Tony Morton, Colin Dye, and others who cover streams of churches. Many of these ministries are located in the London vicinity, and most of these leaders oversee between 200 and 300 churches that enjoy a tremendous spirit of unity and colaboring in Christ. Terry Virgo, for instance, organized a week of revival services and 21,000 people turned up. That's a big gathering of God's people, especially in England. Many of the church leaders in the northeast sector of England began to desire this same kind of unity and apostolic covering for their region, and some of them asked me to consider establishing this kind of apostolic covering and organization, although their ministries were located some distance away.

It is very flattering when people come to you with the purest of motives and ask you to cover them apostolicly. This occurred after we had finally fulfilled God's first entrustment for East Sunderland. At that time Lois and I did not pastor any single local congregation, so we were certainly free to tackle this kind of project, but the Lord started talking to me about *entrustment*. He said, "I want you to keep it simple. You started simple; now don't get complicated. Keep it simple. Keep with those things that have been entrusted to you."

How many times have you agreed to a thing before you heard from the Lord on it? Well, I had already verbally agreed to provide apostolic leadership to some brethren in Lancashire (an area located in other parts of northern England). Yet the Lord spoke to my heart and reminded me of the entrustment He had given me: to establish an apostolic base in northeast England. From this base we were to send out our international ministry that would take the renewal refreshing and revival fire of God into the world, and mercy and mission to the poor. I had only one choice. I had to write my brethren and tell them that I had spoken too soon, and that I couldn't step beyond the entrustments God had given me. It was embarrassing in a way, but I had already learned the hard way just how difficult it is to handle an enticement instead of an entrustment. No one in his right mind wants to get out on a limb without God! I was confident that God would entrust the leadership of my Lancashire brethren to a faithful man He had raised up for the task, and I was determined to stay within the boundaries God had set for me.

If you realize that you have failed to handle God's entrustment to you because you were distracted by enticements along the way, it isn't too late to correct your course. God will come alongside any man or woman who wants to step back into obedience. Pray this prayer with me before we go on:

Dear Father in Heaven, search our hearts and know our ways. If there is any evil way in us, if we have stepped away from Your divine entrustments to take up enticements, reveal the truth to us today. As our Father, we ask You to correct and rebuke us today so that we might be healed and restored. We invite You to be a Father to us as Your children, and to chastise us as any earthly father would do. Restore us to obedience today, that we might handle those things that You have placed within our hearts. We submit ourselves to You, Lord. If in anything we have said or done we have sounded proud or arrogant, please forgive us. We stand before You in humility of spirit and ask You, Lord, to forgive us of our sins in Jesus' name, especially if we have done anything to discredit Your name. We want to be like Your Son who, through total obedience, glorified Your holy name in the earth.

*We say **no** to those things that will keep us down and exiled in the desert. We say **no** to the enticements that seem good at the time, and we say **yes** to the entrustment You have given us. We want to soar on the wings of Your Spirit to the place You want us to be—regardless of our nation, people group, culture, or society. Lift us above our obstacles and shortcomings and into that righteous river that will literally take us around the world with the good news. We repent before You today, and we ask You to come again as the God of the second chance. Be the God of the third, fourth, and fifth chance.*

Put Your arms around us and restore us as You once did with Peter. And may You receive all the glory, Lord. Please continue to put Your entrustments in our hands that we might handle them for You as faithful and trustworthy stewards. In Jesus' name, amen.

Chapter 5

The Shout
That Stops God

Very often, when television screens around the world flash announcements from NASA, the U.S. space exploration agency, you will hear a spokesman talk about a critical "window of opportunity." If a dangerous weather front is advancing toward a space shuttle launch site, then the experts calculate a window of opportunity, that time frame in which everything should be launch-ready on the spacecraft, when the position of the earth's axis and target zone is in proper alignment, and the latest possible launch time before the bad weather comes crashing in on the site, making the launch impossible. The only opportunity that shuttle and its astronauts have to escape the pull of gravity will fall somewhere within that critical window of opportunity. There is no allowance made for delay or hesitation.

There is a man in England who is very successful businessman. He owns an airline along with some other enterprises, and has become tremendously popular throughout the nation. One day he decided to circumnavigate the world in a hot air balloon.

I know that sounds romantic, but the only way you can do that is to take a hot air balloon as high as you can in hopes of hitting the jet stream. If you manage this, then you have to hope and pray that the jet stream will take you where you want to go because up there you are simply "along for the ride." It's pretty difficult to get a balloon high enough to tap the jet stream due to the extreme cold and scarcity of oxygen at that height. High-altitude balloonists have to pack support equipment such as oxygen tanks, radio and navigation gear, and heavily insulated clothing in the balloon gondola just to survive, and the more weight you have, the harder it is for the balloon to escape the lower atmosphere. On top of everything else, storms, shifting winds, and rapidly changing atmospheric conditions can quickly put you in harm's way even on the best of days. This man had to find his window of opportunity, weather-wise, to catch the jet stream or his mission would surely fail.

The Church has never seen a day like this day before. I have been told that 140,000 people receive Christ as Savior and are added to the Church every 24 hours. This has never happened before on this magnitude.

It is estimated that 26,000 people get saved every day in Communist China alone—a nation where it is a criminal act to profess Christ! One of the provinces of China can claim something that cannot be claimed by any state or region in the United States, Great Britain, or any other major Western nation—90 percent of the population of China's Hunan province is Christian. More people on this planet have become Christians *in the last ten years* than in all of Church history combined! The Kingdom of God is on the rise.

I used to pray, "Lord, give us another Pentecost." But then I discovered that every single day we get *46 times* the Church growth experienced by the disciples on the Day of Pentecost! God has given us a unique window of opportunity in history. We must be determined not to miss this launch window and let a divine opportunity pass us by! We are compelled to do everything we can do to take hold of that for which Jesus Christ has taken hold of us (see Phil. 3:12).

Blind and Begging

Now they came to Jericho. As He went out of Jericho with His disciples and a great multitude, blind Bartimaeus, the son of Timaeus, sat by the road begging. And when he heard that it was Jesus of Nazareth, he began to cry out and say, "Jesus, Son of David, have mercy on me!" Then many warned him to be quiet; but he cried out all the more, "Son of David, have mercy on me!" So Jesus stood still and commanded him to be called. Then they called the blind man, saying to him, "Be of good cheer. Rise, He is calling you." And throwing aside his garment, he rose and came to Jesus. So Jesus answered and said to him, "What do you want Me to do for you?" The blind man said to Him, "Rabboni, that I may receive my sight." Then Jesus said to him, "Go your way; your faith has made you well." And immediately he received his sight and followed Jesus on the road (Mark 10:46-52).

We are seeing the beginning of an unprecedented harvest of souls in our day. For many years, though, the Church has been much like Bartimaeus—*blind and begging.* Unlike the man described in the Gospel of Mark, most of our suffering and lack has been self-inflicted through ignorance, stubbornness, or outright rebellion. Some of us managed to be thankful, but many did not. We were proud, self-serving prodigal sons in our attitudes and blind beggars in our prayers, works, and faith.

The tiny world that Bartimaeus occupied was deprived of vision and entirely too predictable, as was ours not too long ago. Day after dreary day, he was led by the hand of another to a certain spot on the side of the road *outside* the city of Jericho. It was to a place no one else wanted that this unwanted beggar was taken each day. He came to know that barren roadside spot so well that he could pinpoint the exact location of every little stone, bump, and mound of dust. He knew every smell and sound common to his world, and though he couldn't see, he still knew everything there was to know about that little area around the gate of Jericho. Every day, the people who came in and left the city gate heard Bartimaeus pleading for money and declaring to everyone within hearing range, "I am but a poor, blind beggar. Have pity on me. Alms for the poor."

One day something different happened. A divine window of opportunity opened up right in front of the blind man. The Scriptures tell us that Bartimaeus allowed Jesus to walk right past him on His way into Jericho, while engaged in a deep conversation with 12 other men. Though the group was relatively large, Bartimaeus didn't know the significance of their presence. Yet something important must have happened while Jesus was in Jericho. The Bible only tells us that He came in and went out, but when Jesus passed by blind Bartimaeus the second time, He was surrounded by a noisy and excited crowd, not just the 12 disciples.

Rumors of what was happening in the city because of Jesus even filtered through the city gate to the blind beggar— I'd like to think that Jesus was doing what He always did:

healing the sick and doing good. Now when you are a blind beggar, you are only interested in one thing. I think perhaps the first question Bartimaeus may have asked was, "Has He healed any blind eyes?" If they said, "Oh yeah, He heals the blind." The second question would be this: "Who is He, anyway?" "Well, actually He's calling Himself—or at least some say—that He is the Son of God. Others actually claim that He is a descendant from the lineage of David himself."

Now when you are blind and you are begging, you quickly deal with the theological problem. When you need your eyes opened and there is a man nearby who actually does this, and He wants to be called "the son of David," He's got it! "He likes to call Himself 'the son of man.'" "Well, that's all right too." Bartimaeus didn't even blink when he heard a really wild report, "Well, I heard He told some Pharisees, 'Before Abraham was, I AM.'" "No problem—if He really heals blind eyes."

If you are dry, barren, desperate, and needing a touch from God, then you won't really have very many questions when you hear about a nearby river where you can jump in and be refreshed, renewed, and revived.

What if the blind man had asked, "How does He open blind eyes?" "Well, Bartimaeus, you might not want to hear about that part." "Oh no, I really do." "You might not want to know that he spits in people's eyes, or spits in mud and slaps it on your eyes." "Really? Well, ask Him to spit right here!" You are not afraid of being offended when you're blind and begging.

I Want to Spit in Your Eye

Sometimes you have to let God spit in your face if you want to be healed. In 1986, Lois and I had already been leading an outreach work in Sunderland for nearly a year, and as Christmas approached we were looking forward to the birth of our third baby. Two weeks before Christmas, Lois had a detailed dream in which she give birth to a still-born child in the hospital and held our son in her arms with tears flowing down her face. Strangely enough, she also saw herself still pregnant as she walked with me out of the hospital and into a great harvest field.

A week later Lois and I were lying in bed thinking about the soon-coming birth of our child. We decided that if the baby was a boy, then we would name him Matthew (which means "gift of God"). That very night Lois was rushed to the hospital and every detail of her frightening dream came to pass exactly as she had seen it (although it would take us eight years to understand the meaning of the last part of the dream).

Just before we lost Matthew, I was driving along in the car listening to a tape of a young Welsh gospel singer and fiery youth evangelist named Ray Bevan. The Holy Spirit suddenly spoke to my heart and said, "Invite this man to minister to your church. He'll bless you." As soon as I got home, I called the man and arranged for him to come to Sunderland in February to minister to the church and visit local schools. In the meantime, we lost Matthew and nearly lost Lois when she began to hemorrhage uncontrollably. It devastated our lives and nearly ended our ministry. We buried little Matthew, and a few days later I told our small congregation, "There might be 101 reasons why it happened, but come what may, we are going to serve the Lord. And although we do not understand the whys and wherefores, we love the Lord more than we have ever done before."

I thought I was a good person, and I didn't realize that bad things can happen to good people too. Although I was determined to walk with God, I still questioned Him and wondered why our little baby had died. Lois was critically wounded in both body and spirit. She was chronically ill for two long years marked by constant hospital stays and endless months spent confined to bedrest in our room. I looked after two daughters, ministered in the church, and tried to keep my head above the rising waters. It was just a tough time.

I remember calling Ray Bevan and saying, "Listen, this isn't a good time for you to come, Ray. I would like to cancel the appointment." His only reply was, "No, I really think that I should still come." So I said, "Look, this is not a good time for you to come. Come later in the year. But right now, I'm just not ready to receive you. Ray, I wouldn't even be with you in the school meetings. I'd have to put you with somebody else." It didn't do any good. Eventually I said, "Listen, Ray, you know we've just lost a little baby boy. My wife is ill in the house, and I'm totally shattered and devastated. I just don't know where I am. Really, *this is just not a good time to come.*"

Do you know what Ray said? "Ken, I'm sorry to hear it, but I still think that I should come." This man did not rank as one of the most sensitive individuals in my universe at that time. Despite my best efforts, nobody else would have him, so Ray Bevan ended up staying in our house that February. Now knowing what I had told Ray, how would you prepare for a stay with Lois and I less than two months after we'd lost our only son in stillbirth? You might want to take a course in inner healing, or perhaps you'd take one of those deep ministry courses so you could minister the life of God to our broken hearts....

Well, Ray didn't know anything about that. He came into our home moving a hundred miles an hour and speaking in tongues at a tornado pace. He didn't even make an attempt to "tone down" to accommodate our grief and heartbroken condition. That guy spoke in tongues everywhere he went! He did it in the living room, he did it in the bedroom, and he even did it in the bathroom (which was next to our bedroom, naturally). I *never* had to wonder where Ray Bevan was at any minute of the day. He was all charged up with no place to go. Meanwhile, Lois and I were just trying to make it through each day without suffering a total collapse mentally, physically, and spiritually.

Ray just kept asking me where my wife was, and I kept telling him, "She's sick, Ray." (I confess that at the time I felt like saying "She is sick of *you*," but I didn't.) One day Ray and I were talking on the landing just outside the bedroom where Lois was. Suddenly Ray turned toward me and reached out to knock on the bedroom door! Lois answered, "Yes," and Ray quickly poked his head in and said, "Do you have any hair spray?" (I've given up trying to figure that one out, but today I praise God for Ray's boldness and obedience to God's voice.)

"No," Lois said with a puzzled look. "I don't have any hair spray. I have no need of hair spray in this condition," she said, pulling at her hair as she lay in bed. Ray must have taken that warm answer as an open invitation because he just edged on into our room. So I followed him in to see what else would happen. Ray sat down on the end of the bed and started talking to both of us as if we were drinking tea in the back garden. That was about all I could stand, so in frustration I said, "*Ray, what are you on?*" I should have known he was waiting for me to ask. "I've been to Harere in Zimbabwe [Africa]," he said. "I've been to a Fire Conference."

That caught me off guard. "A fire conference? What is that?" Once again I had stepped into the noose. Ray said, "It's Reinhard Bonnke's conference. That's when he pulls all the evangelists together in a Fire Conference."

"Oh yeah? What happened?" I asked. "Ken, you wouldn't believe it," he said. "I went expecting everything that God had for me. I put a funnel on my head and just said, 'God, pour it in, pour it in.' Reinhard came over to me as I stood in line and he put his hand right here. Then I went down under the power. I got filled with the anointing," Ray continued, "and this is what I'm like."

Then Ray looked at me and said, "You know, Ken, next year you need to go to the Fire Conference." I had to admit I was interested. When Ray told me the next conference was scheduled to be held in Frankfurt, Germany, I told him I thought I would go. I sensed that the Lord was telling me, "You go. I sent this man to send you there."

Looking for Fire at a Conference

Twelve months later, Lois wasn't getting much better, but the church was beginning to see some progress. Lois and I made plans to go to Frankfurt, Germany, for the conference. We were scheduled to leave at midnight on the night before the conference to catch our flight out of London. I had arranged to send the controlled drugs Lois needed through customs, and I had nurses waiting at the other end of our flight to inject Lois with her drugs and provide other things she needed. We were all set to go, but at one minute to midnight she looked at me and said, "Ken, I just can't go. I'm too sick, and I'm too afraid as well. I don't want to leave this country. You go. Just get your mom to come around and sit with me. I'll be fine. You need to go."

I felt so alone on the flight to Frankfurt, and my heart was breaking. I said to God, "If You don't meet me at this conference, I'm finished. I'll ask the police force if they will have me back. I'll find another job. I'm finished." (This was Nachon's threshing floor for Ken Gott.) Reinhard was there, and so was Ray McCaulay, another great Christian leader from South Africa. They were praying for people and people were being blessed.

There was another guy there called Benny Hinn, but the minute I saw him I decided I didn't like him. (You should know that I love Benny today, and that his wife and mine are best friends.) I didn't like the way he dressed. I didn't like his accent either, or the way he seemed to be full of show. I just didn't like anything at all about this Benny Hinn character. Every time Benny Hinn stood up to minister, I would be muttering under my breath, "Let him get on with his thing so Reinhard will appear."

The first meeting was wonderful. There were 5,000 delegates there, and Reinhard began to pray for people. I took my place in line and waited for him to come by. I had put Ray Bevan's "funnel" of expectancy on my head and everything, but for some reason he stopped before he got to me and then he went off somewhere else. In my heart, I cried out, "God! Why?"

The next day I put that "funnel" on once more, but the same thing happened again! This went on all week long, and through it all I endured the Benny Hinn moments, all the while hoping for my special Reinhard Bonnke moment. In the next to the last meeting, I thought my moment "in the fire" had arrived. It was unbelievable. I'll never forget it. I took my place in line, and the man of God kept moving closer as he prayed and blessed the people. *He'll surely get to me this time*, I thought. But it was almost like I was invisible! He actually missed me again!

In the last meeting of the conference, I still had my hopes up. I had been touched just enough in the meetings to feel a little bit better. I was confident that God had something for me. I knew He had sent me to Frankfurt, Germany, to receive something more than I'd received up to that point. The atmosphere was electric, and praise and worship were wonderful. I remember watching a 17-year-old girl walk down the aisle with a woman in her arms. She just dumped the woman on the platform and walked away, and Reinhard looked down at this woman who was just skin and bones. She looked like she was going to die at any second.

Reinhard Bonnke told the crowd, "Speak in tongues. Begin to pray in the Spirit." Meanwhile, I thought to myself, *That was a good move. Get everybody involved.* So we all began to pray in tongues and Reinhard tells the woman at his feet, "Woman, when I pray for you, you will not die, but live in Jesus' name!" *Whoaaaaa. Five thousand people. Video going all over the world. I hope this works!*

Reinhard looked up and said, "Pray! Pray for this woman." I prayed, but I didn't pray for the woman—I prayed for Reinhard. I liked him, and besides, he hadn't prayed for me yet. We all prayed and Reinhard took the woman by the hand and lifted her up as he said, "Woman, walk in Jesus' name!" She stood up and began to walk, and a blanket of power seemed to come on her. I could see strength filling every fiber of her being. First she began to walk, then she jumped, and the teenage girl jumped up and hugged her mother. It was fantastic, and the place went wild.

I thought, *Oh God, I would love to have that anointing.* Right at that moment when everything had reached the pinnacle of spiritual excitement, Reinhard Bonnke turned to…yes…Benny Hinn. He said, "Benny, come and pray for the sick," and I thought, *Reinhard, you were doing so well. We don't need Benny to pray for the sick.* If you don't know it already, let me tell you that Benny Hinn doesn't just pray for the sick. I didn't know it at the time, but Benny has a proven pattern that he always follows in his ministry, because that is the way God has chosen to work through him. He took his jacket off and stood at the front of the platform and led the conference in seemingly endless renditions of the chorus, "Hallelujah, Hallelujah." We sang it loud and we sang it soft. We sang it quick and we sang it slow. We sang it with our arms up and we sang it with our arms down. In fact, we sang it for a full 20 minutes. And I was offended. *Why doesn't he just do what he was told to do, pray for the sick,* I fumed.

My Time Came

The endless chorus finally ended and Benny received some words of knowledge and prayed for the sick. Some people were healed, but I remained unimpressed. Then he said, "Okay, I want to pray now for the English pastors." You wouldn't believe what happened the minute he said it. English pastors ran to the platform from every part of that building! They ran from the top corner, and from the left and the right. They even ran over chairs like idiots in their mad rush to get to the front. And I beat the lot of them.

Since I got there first, I took my position on the corner of the platform. My eyes were closed in good Pentecostal fashion, but I could hear Benny Hinn saying to the men as he passed them, "Take it, take it, take it, take it," and I was thinking, *I'm offended, I'm offended, I'm offended, I'm offended.*

Suddenly everything became quiet for some reason. There wasn't a sound in the place. Then I heard Benny say, "Young man." I opened my eyes and noticed with a shock that he was looking right at me and standing about ten yards away. "Are you an English pastor?" he asked. "Yes, I am," I replied.

"Come here," he said. When I began to walk toward him, I felt something I'd never felt before. I felt the tangible anointing of God. This "field" of anointing measured a meter (almost a yard) off the ground, and the closer I got to Benny, the stronger it became. By the time I reached the area right in front of him I was vibrating like a leaf. He just looked at me and said "Take it." Slap. "Take it." That was when I fell down, and that was also when I realized that the field of anointing may have only come up to my knees when I was standing up, but when I fell down, I was "baptized" in it. (I also realized that when we are all on the carpet, we all have about the same stature.)

Benny Hinn captured my attention all over again when he said, "Okay, pick him up again." There were some large, well-built men standing on each side of me, and they moved closer as Benny did exactly what I hoped he wouldn't—he blew right in my face. I was about to get really offended, but Benny's breath just went all over my body and I fell down again! It got worse. I heard him tell the muscular men towering over me, "Pick him up again." By this time, I was shaking like a leaf, my hair was on end, and I was vibrating under the power of God. He looked right at me and said, "Young man, from this moment on you will never be the same again. Take it." And I fell down for the count.

Benny was right: I was never the same. He let me sprawl there in front of everybody for about 30 minutes, and during that half hour, God put His hand right into my chest and healed my broken heart. He put me back together again, and when I stood up I was a different man. I was healed. I still didn't have an explanation for why we lost Matthew, but I knew that God had done something very powerful in my life. I went to that conference wanting Reinhard Bonnke to put his hand on the top of my head, like he had for Ray Bevan. I wanted God's anointing and blessing to come to me through Reinhard, but God chose to use a man whom I had found to be offensive. He chose to transform my life through the ministry of a man who cut straight across the grain of my European culture and everything else I believed in. Let me tell you, those who are never offended at Benny Hinn are the wheelchair-bound, the blind, and the dying.

In the end, I was so hungry that I cut through the offense and stood in front of the man whom God had chosen to minister life and wholeness to me in that hour. I'm so glad I ran out of my seat. I'm so glad that I didn't cling to my "right to be offended." The truth is that I didn't have a lot of options. I could either stay back in my seat and remain broken, hurt, wounded, and ineffective; or I could obey God and run to the front so "God's choice" for that day could pray for me. (Incidentally, it was Benny whom God used months later to minister my wife's healing.)

Never Give Up

Bartimaeus didn't have any options either. He was blind and begging, and the only man in his day who could heal blind eyes—the one who called Himself the Son of God—was passing by. "Son of David, have mercy on me!" Bartimaeus made up his mind. He knew that he had a tiny window of opportunity that was about to open up. It would only take Jesus between 10 and 20 seconds to walk by with the noisy crowd. I think Bartimaeus just made up his mind to stop the Healer at any cost. He wasn't going to be passed up again. I can almost see him asking people every 15 minutes or so, "Is He coming yet? Have you heard anything from the city?" Again and again he was told, "No, He's in the middle of the city teaching in the synagogue. No, He's in the Temple. What are you asking for? No, He's with the Pharisees."

Then the moment came when he heard the rumor—Jesus was about to leave Jericho! I think Bartimaeus' heart started to pound, and he began to perspire. *This is my only chance. I can't blow it, this guy and His healing power are all I've got.* He anxiously waited for the right time, straining to hear every sound of His approach. Timing was so important. He heard the noise long before Jesus and the crowd surrounding Him passed through the city gate. The people around Him were probably pushing and screaming out for the Lord's attention. They wanted Him to touch them, and the disciples were just as determined to keep the people a respectable distance away from their Master.

So Jesus passed through the city gate leaving Jericho while a blind beggar tensely waited to seize his window of opportunity. At the last possible moment, the beggar filled his lungs with air until he felt he would burst. Just as Jesus walked within earshot, the forgotten beggar on the side of the road shouted at the top of his voice, "**J-e-s-u-u-u-s, Son of David, have mercy on me!**"

Jesus didn't seem to hear the beggar shout the first time around, but some of the people did. They were quick to put the beggar in his place by roughly telling him to shut up. They considered him to be a "second-rate" person who didn't deserve Jesus' attention (aren't we all?). But it didn't do any good. I love what the Bible says, "Then many warned him to be quiet; *but he cried out all the more*" (Mk. 10:48a). So Bartimaeus just got worse. He filled his lungs again and yelled at the top of his voice in a tone filled with desperation, "**J-e-s-u-u-u-s, Son of David, have mercy on me!**"

It was the shout that stopped God. What did Jesus hear? Did He hear a blind man who was simply shouting louder than everybody else, or did He hear the cry of a desperate heart that was determined not to let hope and opportunity pass by again? Do we really have to stop God? Do we really have to have that kind of determination to stop Jesus? Isn't this a day of grace and mercy when God wants to lavish His blessing upon the Church? God does want to bless us, but He always responds to the hunger and faith in the cries of a desperate heart. He wants to know how desperate we are to stop Him. Are you desperate enough to stop Him at your church? Are you desperate enough to stop Him at your city, state, or province? Are you desperate enough to stop God for your nation? Are you desperate enough to stop God for yourself and your family? Is there a cry of desperation in your heart that cuts through every other noise and distraction? God hears every cry that comes from a desperate heart.

> *So Jesus stood still and commanded him to be called. Then they called the blind man, saying to him, "Be of good cheer. Rise, He is calling you." And throwing aside his garment, he rose and came to Jesus. So Jesus answered and said to him, "What do you want Me to do for you?" The blind man said to Him, "Rabboni, that I may receive my sight." Then Jesus said to him, "Go your way; your faith has made you well." And immediately he received his sight and followed Jesus on the road (Mark 10:49-52).*

The Shout That Stopped God

There is a shout of a desperate heart that will stop God at this window of opportunity in the world. Only a few years ago revivals were confined to the history books. Now you have a choice of revival hot spots that you may go to visit. Unprecedented things are happening all over the world. You can shout the shout, not necessarily loud in volume, but in a desperation and determination of heart that will stop God in your life, church, city, or nation.

Bartimaeus was a desperate man with only one shot at receiving his sight. His response was so loud and so powerful that his shout will forever be remembered as "the shout that stopped God." I love Eugene Peterson's rendering in *The Message* of what happened next:[1]

Jesus stopped in his tracks. "Call him over." They called him. "It's your lucky day! Get up! He's calling you to come!" (Mark 10:49)

The Bible says that the moment Bartimaeus reached Jesus, the Lord asked him what He could do for him. Once you stop Jesus with a shout of desperation, He is going to ask you what you want. If you have stopped Him with the cries from your heart as you read this chapter, what do you want Him to do for you? What do you *really* want? It almost always boils down to something that can only be found in God Himself.

"J-e-e-e-s-u-u-u-s!

"J-e-e-e-s-u-u-u-s!

"J-e-e-e-s-u-u-u-s!, Son of David, have m-e-e-e-r-c-y-y-y-y on m-e-e-e!"

You'll hear other voices in the background. You'll hear jealous voices, concerned voices, and scoffing voices saying, "Get up! Just be quiet. Be quiet! Now get up and stop looking so foolish. Get up, get up! We don't do that in church. We don't do that in public. Get a grip on yourself."

"**J-e-e-e-s-u-u-u-s!**"

"Get up! I'm serious—get up and *be quiet.* ***Be quiet!***"

"**J-e-e-e-s-u-u-u-s! Son of David, have m-e-e-e-r-c-y-y-y-y on m-e-e-e!**"

"Shut up! Shut up and be quiet. Please, just be quiet. *Be quiet.*"

"**J-e-e-e-s-u-u-u-s! Son of David, have m-e-e-e-r-c-y-y-y-y on m-e-e-e!**"

"Be quiet. This is not for you. You don't have the education and status for this. This is not for your area—your people aren't ready yet. They don't need it (*and they don't deserve it either*).

"Be quiet. Weren't you taught anything? You are to behave with dignity in church. You will not be radical, and above all you will not make noise. You will be insignificant and impotent. You will be powerless against the forces of darkness, and you will not win. No, you will not stop God. Just sit in your pews and sing songs like a good nominal Christian. Don't change, because everyone knows change is bad."

"**J-e-e-e-s-u-u-u-s! Son of David, have m-e-e-e-r-c-y-y-y-y on m-e-e-e!**"

We will be silent no more! We will not be put down. We will shout until God stops in His tracks. We will shout until God stops in our city. We will not be silenced until God stops to ask, "What do you want Me to do for you?" Have mercy on us, Lord.

Endnote

1 Eugene H. Peterson, *The Message: New Testament with Psalms and Proverbs* (Colorado Springs, CO: NavPress Publishing Group, 1995), p. 117.

Chapter 6

Answering the Prayers of the Lost

My life and ministry were deeply affected the day I heard David Ruis, the anointed psalmist and minister from Canada, tell the story of how the Lord called him to begin an outreach work in Winnipeg, Ontario. Instead of renting a hotel meeting room and advertising his meetings, he said that he felt he should simply gather a few people from the neighborhood for an informal meeting in his front room. His "gathering" was just a little different from most because his guests included prostitutes, homosexuals, and drug addicts from nearby low-income housing units.

He said that he began the meeting by saying, "Do you know why I've pulled you together? I want to pray for you." David was sure this would be an unusual idea to his unusual guests, but each and every one of them said, "We pray too." David was astounded and amazed. "You pray?" he said. "Yeah, we pray." He had to know more, so he asked, "What do you pray about? Who do you pray to?"

"We pray to anyone who will listen," they replied. One said, "Every time I put my head on my pillow, I pray to anyone who might be out there, 'God, get me out of this hellhole! Change my situation and my circumstances. God, bring my kids home, and keep them safe tonight on the streets.' " Some of them prayed things like, "God, do something about my husband who is abusing me and my children." David said he began to see that it wasn't *his prayers* that led him to that neighborhood in Winnipeg; it was *the desperate prayers of sinners* that moved God to send him there.

I couldn't shake the question those people asked David Ruis: "We pray every single night. Wouldn't you if you lived where we have to live?" Then it dawned on me that the people living in the ghetto-type apartments surrounding our church building in East Sunderland were the same kind of people. They probably prayed every night too. The Holy Spirit just wouldn't let up on me, and I kept asking myself, *How many mothers in East Sunderland have laid their heads on tear-stained pillows tonight to pray, "God, if You are out there, do something about my situation. Do something about my girl and my boy. Take them off drugs, God"?*

I knew there were children going to bed all around my church office who would put their heads on their pillows and pray, "Please don't let him come into my room tonight. God, if You are there, don't let him come into my room tonight and do those terrible things. I can't take it anymore. Please, God, I've heard about You at school. They say that You are out there somewhere. If You are, then don't let him touch me that way." It shook me so and cut me to the heart when I pictured hundreds of little girls and boys speaking out into the air to a God they can only hope exists.

I could almost see a woman with a terribly bruised face hesitate before she put her head on her pillow. Before she closed her eyes, she said, "If there is a God out there at all, if You really exist...if You are out there, then please do something about my husband and his drinking. He's really a good man at heart, God, but when he gets drunk he just goes crazy and he always hurts me. I'm afraid he's going to kill me some day, God. Please, God, if You exist at all, then don't let him come home drunk tonight. I don't think I can stand another beating like the last one." And then she closed her eyes and went to sleep in her empty apartment.

I saw another image of an 18-year-old young man who was running with the gangs. He knew there was something a lot better out there, and he knew he could achieve things. He also knew that he was running with the gangs because of peer pressure. He didn't want to be an outcast, but all the time that he was doing drugs and participating in violent acts, he didn't like it. He was sick of feeling ashamed every time he went back home after a run with the gang. I can still hear him praying, "God, if You are out there at all, then get me out of this hellhole. Get me out of the gangs. Break me out of the drug racket and the violence." He knew that if he had a chance, he'd go to college and make something of his life. With no hope left, all he can do is shout into the air, "God, if You are there at all, do something."

These prayers are multiplied thousands upon thousands of times in the lives of people who feel hopelessly trapped in difficult or dangerous situations. I know that God hears every one of them. It is God's answer to those prayers that caught me off guard the most. God is saying to the searching sinner, "Yes, I heard your prayer and I'm working on the answer and solution to your problem." God's answer is

His field and *His building. His answer is you.* I was shocked
the day I realized that one of God's answers to the prayers
of sinners in East Sunderland came in the form of a young
couple named Ken and Lois Gott!

An Entrustment for East Sunderland

Now I knew why God gave me the entrustment to build
a community church right in the middle of one of the
toughest neighborhoods in East Sunderland. We managed
to build a beautiful church building, and every night for
over two and a half years, we saw the fire of God come in renewal and revival. Hundreds of thousands of people joined
us there for glorious revival meetings in the very shadow of
the apartment buildings where women, children, gang
members, and hopeless people of every description were
mouthing desperate prayers to a God they hoped was listening. Meanwhile, we were building a regional church at-
tended by people who lived far from the squalor of East
Sunderland. We came in our suits and nice cars, and we did
what we had to do to preserve our comfortable church culture. Yet even though the church was growing and being
blessed, not one person crossed the street from those apartment complexes to come into our church. It was as though
we were invisible to them— except for our high security
fence and armed security guards.

One day a woman came up to me who had been saved in
the renewal. A Christian for only six months, God was
about to use her to shame me for my apathy and disobedience! She stood right beside me and said, "Ken, what are we
doing about the poor in this city?" (Pastors just love questions like that.) I said, "Well, you know, we take up an offering once in awhile, and we support one or two little
things...but *actually* we're not doing anything."

"But Pastor, this is the coldest winter we've had for a long, long time. There are people out there sleeping in cardboard boxes and we're not doing a thing about it. Why?" I knew why we weren't doing anything about it. It was because I wasn't concerned about the problem. It just wasn't high on my priority list. I had one very serious problem—it was high on the Lord's priority list!

I couldn't help but think of the passage in Isaiah 58 where God says, "Is this not the fast *that I have chosen...?*" (Is. 58:6), along with all the uncomfortable things that follow His question. I thought of the time Jesus shocked the disciples by warning them that the day would come when He would separate the sheep from the goats, saying very uncomfortable things like, "You gave Me food...you gave Me drink...you clothed Me...you visited Me..." (see Mt. 25:31-46). It got worse. I remembered how Jesus launched His earthly ministry by saying, "The Spirit of the Lord is upon Me, because He has anointed Me to preach the gospel to the *poor*" (Lk. 4:18a). Then the apostle Paul got into the act when he gave his report to the Galatian believers about his meeting with the Jerusalem counsel. He said, "They desired only that we should remember the *poor*, the very thing which I also was eager to do" (Gal. 2:10).

I had to admit before God that I didn't have a concern for the poor. In some ways I had produced some conflict with my wife since Lois always loved the poor. She had always worked and ministered among the poor. Then I had to face this young believer who was asking me, "What are we doing?" There was only one thing I could do. I said, "Listen, if you feel we need to be doing something, then go and do it." (That used to work when you were a leader, because in the days before revival most people would forget about any new idea once they found out that it wasn't as easy as they thought.) There was more behind this woman, though, than empty talk. She put together a team of people from the church and the next thing I knew, she was feeding hot meals to 70 homeless, needy, and lonely people on Tuesday afternoon. Not only that, but she had her team members sitting at tables witnessing and sharing the Lord. She was so organized that she came to me asking for permission to launch a second team to serve the needy in our community! Then the Lord spoke to my heart: "Ken, I don't want you to just give her an afternoon—I want you to give this whole building to the community."

"Lord, that wouldn't be fair," I protested. Then I remembered that I'd never seen any place in the Bible that says God is fair. He is always wanting us to deny ourselves, to sacrifice, to go the extra mile. That's not fair! No, but it is just, and it glorifies God. I wasn't quite ready to give up the fight, however. *Well, what about the people who sold their houses just to get this building up? What about all the sacrificial giving? It's not fair for me to say, "I'm sorry, I'm going to give this building to the poor. Get out."*

Then something remarkable happened. By God's grace, I simply released it in my spirit. I was able to say, "Well, Lord, You're going to have to sort it out." (I was about to find out that God took my words seriously.)

God Prepared the Congregation

In July of 1995, one month after the Spirit of God suddenly descended on Brownsville Assembly of God Church in Pensacola, Florida, an Argentine pastor named Ed Silvoso came to Sunderland as a guest speaker. Lois and I had left the country for a much needed vacation, and we had no idea what God was about to do in East Sunderland.

Ed Silvoso had played a key role in the revival that has swept across Argentina and burned continuously for more than a decade.

The first thing he did was confirm that the same atmosphere of revival was in Sunderland that he had felt just before revival hit Argentina, sweeping thousands of souls into the Kingdom of God. When this was relayed to us by telephone, we were excited. We had been richly blessed in renewal and blessing, but we still hadn't seen the dynamic power and evangelistic anointing common to true revival.

The next day a secretary called us to say, "Guess what Ed Silvoso prophesied tonight...he said that the Lord is about to *take down the fence* that surrounds our church property because the local community is about to come in and it will no longer be necessary!" That prophecy gave me more "rest and relaxation" than anything else on my vacation. I was really looking for confirmation of God's unsettling request to give our $880,000 church building to the community, because it wasn't totally paid for yet and we would have no place to go! This prophecy was a strong confirmation.

In September of that year, Wes Campbell came to Sunderland from his home in Kelowna, Canada, to be the keynote speaker for our prophetic conference. Norm Strauss, a worship leader who had also come from Canada, was with us to lead the ministry time. The meetings went well. There was a strong message from Wes the last night, followed by the usual ministry time, and we assumed that the service would follow the pattern of the previous nights. The people who had received ministry would continue in the Lord's presence and "rest" in Him until they were ready to go home. So Lois and I took a number of pastors to a hospitality lounge upstairs and began to pray with them. Suddenly we heard a rising tide of voices shouting, "Fire! Fire!"

We rushed downstairs wondering how and where a fire could have started, but when we reached the first floor we were shocked by what we saw. The weighty Presence of God permeated the entire first floor, and hundreds of people were on their feet with their hands raised in the air. I felt like I was eavesdropping on the miracle of Pentecost! The sound of praise was almost deafening, and spontaneous cries of "Fire!" and "Hallelujah!" punctuated the wall of sound. Then the joy of God descended on everyone and the people began to form a "conga chain" and began to dance! They threw open our high security fire doors and danced right out of the building and into the streets while our surprised security guards gaped and scratched their heads!

Nearly a thousand people emptied out of the building and into the neighborhood in that Holy Ghost chorus line, and then they filed back in through a door on the other side—but only for a moment. It seemed that no one could stay in the building any longer! I believe it was a prophetic moment: God was about to take what was in the church out into the streets. The people were driven to spread their joy to anyone they could find. Some rushed out to the line of waiting taxi cabs and began to witness excitedly to the shocked taxi drivers. Others rushed to their hotels and guest houses to share the gospel with their hosts. Everyone had a compulsive desire to tell others about the Savior, Jesus Christ. All the excitement had a strong effect on the city of Sunderland, and especially on our neighborhood. But the biggest miracle came the following night.

Lois and I were relaxing at home when the phone rang. One of the members of Wes Campbell's team who had stayed behind to work with us was calling from the church building. He said a number of youth from the neighborhood were at the church door asking to come in! In the three and a half years we had been in the new church building, the only thing we experienced when the neighborhood youth showed up was trouble. These gangs had robbed, stolen, and vandalized cars and threatened innocent people. On the rare occasion a few of them had entered the building or showed up at a function, they had rioted or run through the crowd snatching purses and the like. This time they had shown up to come to church. What were we to do?

The Holy Spirit had made His point the night before. He wanted the Presence of God to be taken to the streets and the fence to be taken down. Suddenly, the streets had come to us! As always, God gave us the opportunity to put His prophetic word to the test. We told the worker to open the doors, and later that night we learned that five young people had received Jesus Christ as Lord, and the rest of the youth had behaved perfectly. The youth of Sunderland just kept coming, night after night. We decided to give the street kids the exclusive use of our building on Tuesday and Wednesday nights. Revival was in the air, but one thing remained.

For the Community!

The day came when I had to step out in obedience and trust God for what would come next. I told the congregation of Sunderland Christian Centre, "This church is the wrong kind of church for this building." Then I explained that the Lord was calling the main portion of the congregation to move out and form a city church that would serve the region, and that we would seed those who felt called to bring Christ to the neighborhood as a church-planting congregation. They would form the nucleus of a dynamic, service-oriented community church right there in the building we had built three and a half years ago. And I told the people that God wanted us to give our church building to the community without charge. I was shocked at the positive response I received from the people. God had prepared our hearts ahead of time. Only one question remained now: Where would the new city church be planted? Somehow I knew we were to remain right there in the neighborhood of our first entrustment. Now the prophecy of Isaiah began to take on a new light and significance to me.

> *Is this not the fast that I have chosen: To loose the bonds of wickedness, to undo the heavy burdens, to let the oppressed go free, and that you break every yoke? Is it not to share your bread with the hungry, and that you bring to your house the poor who are cast out; when you see the naked, that you cover him, and not hide yourself from your own flesh? Then your light shall break forth like the morning, your healing shall spring forth speedily, and your righteousness shall go before you; the glory of the Lord shall be your rear guard. Then you shall call, and the Lord will answer; you shall cry, and He will say, "Here I am"... (Isaiah 58:6-9).*

Once I released the building into the Lord's hands, our church started to grow exponentially. As of this writing, the church building is beginning to be transformed into a 24-hour ministry and community center, with people coming and going at all hours of the day and night. Our church family grew in one year to over 1,000 people, but we divided the people into smaller groupings and planted seven churches all over the region, again taking the people outside the building. The revival had begun, and the sacrifice and dedication of the church family was staggering. But one thing was clear: We needed more room. We still owed a good sum on the church building we were giving away, so it was impossible to the practical mind for us to get a loan or mortgage on another facility large enough to meet our needs. We didn't know how we were going to do it, but we had made our choice to obey God and do it anyway.

One night Lois was leading a prayer meeting at the center when she just felt that she should lead the people in a great shout of praise to honor God in advance for His miraculous provision for our need. We didn't know it, but in that exact moment God moved on the heart of two wealthy businessmen (one of whom was a member of the church) to make an incredible investment.

The next day, one of the businessmen came up to me and said, "Have you had a look around Crown House?" He was referring to a vacant ten-story office building located two blocks behind our church. "No, I haven't had a look," I said. "Well, we've had a look," he said, "and my partner and I think you should look at it too." I took his suggestion and looked at the building complex, but as I looked at the towering structure, I thought, *Oh, this is a project and a half.* The building had been built for the British equivalent of the American Internal Revenue Service. When the government decided to close its Sunderland office to consolidate its resources, it carefully mothballed the building and put it on the market. That was four and a half years earlier. On that day, I was thinking, *I'm not really ready to take this on.*

The businessman and I may have walked away from the business tower, but we later found out that neither one of us could get it out of our spirits. It just wouldn't go away. In the meantime, this businessman was quietly pursuing his entrustment from God. When he was standing at the base of the tower after going through the building floor by floor, he estimated the asking price to be around £750,000 ($1.25 million U.S. dollars). He figured he had nothing to lose, so he asked about the price and learned that the government was only asking for £250,000 (about $417,000). He and his partner talked about it and they decided to offer £150,000 ($250,000) for the building, *and the government took it.* In total agreement, the business partners bought the building for cash and then dropped the keys in my hand and said, "That's for you."

God had brought me full circle. From the entrustment He gave me, I went to my struggles to overcome our family tragedies and the obstacles to acquiring the land and building the church building in East Sunderland. He confronted me on my first entrustment and gave me a second chance to be part of His answer to the prayers of the hurting people in one East Sunderland neighborhood. Now the entrustment was fulfilled and He had done it again. When the keys to Crown House were dropped into my hand, a more difficult and larger entrustment was deposited with me as well. I had laid down my dream of a megachurch and given my own church to seven trusted pastors, but I believe that because of this obedience, God took us to the world.

Chapter 7

An Anointed
Amateur in the Field

When the move of God began in Sunderland in 1994, I discovered that God wanted me to strip away my professional ways and become an "anointed amateur in the field" once again.

Perhaps the most important question any of us can ask is this: "If God didn't show up, how much of my church service, ministry, and personal lifestyle would continue to roll along untouched and unhindered?" If your honest answer is "Most of it," then you need to realize that everything that remains after God is gone is carried by something *other than* God, and disaster is just around the corner. This is what happened to David. Do you really want to function on the leftovers after God has left the scene?

A Professional Celebration

When David was finally crowned king of Israel and had defeated the Philistines who immediately rose up to challenge him, the first thing he wanted to do was to bring the ark of God back home. He was riding a wave of success. His dreams had finally come true. The return of the ark to Jerusalem after its capture by the Philistines and a 20-year stay in Gibeah would mark his finest hour.

Again David gathered all the choice men of Israel, thirty thousand. And David arose and went with all the people who were with him from Baale Judah to bring up from there the ark of God... (2 Samuel 6:1-2).

David the professional king called in 30,000 *professional* men. These were his heroes, his hand-picked brave hearts who all had military ribbons on their chests. They represented the best professionals he could find. Everything was looking good and the parade and celebration party was about to begin.

So they set the ark of God on a new cart, and brought it out of the house of Abinadab, which was on the hill; and Uzzah and Ahio, the sons of Abinadab, drove the new cart. And they brought it out of the house of Abinadab, which was on the hill, accompanying the ark of God; and Ahio went before the ark. Then David and all the house of Israel played music before the Lord on all kinds of instruments of fir wood, on harps, on stringed instruments, on tambourines, on sistrums, and on cymbals. And when they came to Nachon's threshing floor, Uzzah put out his hand to the ark of God and took hold of it, for the oxen stumbled. Then the anger of the Lord was aroused against Uzzah, and God struck him there for his error; and he died there by the ark of God. And David became angry because of the Lord's outbreak against Uzzah; and he called the name of the place Perez Uzzah to this day. David was afraid of the Lord that day; and he said, "How can the ark of the Lord come to me?" So

David would not move the ark of the Lord with him into the City of David; but David took it aside into the house of Obed-Edom the Gittite (2 Samuel 6:3-10).

The ark of the covenant was a type and shadow of the Presence of God carried among men. David wanted to have the Presence of God in its rightful place, in Jerusalem. His motives were pure and his heart's desire was godly, but he tried to do things his way instead of God's way. Something had changed in the heart of the shepherd boy who was chosen because he would do all that the Lord asked him to do. It has been said that David never went into a major battle without first seeking God's direction, which explains why he was so successful on the battlefield. In this case, David forgot to follow his proven path to God's favor. He acted before he sought God's will. He thought he would honor God by transporting the ark of the covenant on a new cart for the triumphant parade along the 9-mile (15 km) route from Baale Judah (or Kirjath Jearim) to Jerusalem.

David had a habit of doing everything with exuberance. The Bible account paints a picture of thousands of people showing up for the event. It almost seems like David had issued a royal decree that everybody had to get out of their houses and bring anything that would make a lot of noise. "We're going to worship God! I want you singers out there; I want every dancer out there ready to dance. I want the kids out there—in fact, I want the entire nation to come to this party as the Presence of God is returned to its rightful place!"

That new cart was probably the best-looking vehicle in the country, and David assigned his best professional men to watch it. It turns out they are Uzzah and Ahio, two men who grew up in the house of their father, Abinadab—the host whose house was home to the ark for two decades. These men aren't unfamiliar with the ark. Maybe that's the problem—perhaps they became just a little too familiar with it. Regardless, when David assigned them to guard the ark, they were probably told, "You guard that ark. If it falls off that cart, I'm blaming you."

Then the music starts and the party begins. The noise could probably be heard for miles as the long procession traveled slowly over the hills and plains toward Jerusalem. There is joy in the nation, and everyone is celebrating the return of God's Presence to Jerusalem.

At a Rough Spot

Then they came to a place the Bible calls "Nachon's threshing floor" (2 Sam. 6:6). Evidently the procession passed right over this threshing floor. A threshing floor is naturally uneven and rough—that is the reason it is useful for forcefully separating the seed from the chaff of grain. This makes for an unstable road surface for carts and animals. There is another factor here too—there was probably some leftover grain in the hollows of the floor that may very well have been an irresistible temptation for the oxen pulling the cart. According to the Scripture, the ark was shaken on the new cart by the oxen, not necessarily by the rough floor. As far as you and I are concerned, we land on Nachon's threshing floor when we encounter a time of testing or a place of trial, temptation, and uncertainty.

God is going to test the vessels and carriers of His anointing, not the anointing itself. He knows what His Presence is made of—it is the carrier or vehicle that is shaky and sometimes unacceptable to Him. This present-day renewal or revival will come to Nachon's threshing floor—if it hasn't already done so. God will test it for what it is. He will shake us to see what we're using to carry His blessing back to our homes, neighborhoods, and nations.

When the joyful procession and new cart carrying the ark of God came to the threshing floor, the oxen caused the new cart to shake and it appeared as if the Presence of God was about to fall off! Uzzah didn't think about it—he just stretched out his hand to steady it like David asked him to do, and when he did it, God killed him. How many people will try to carry the fire and anointing of God's Presence in this revival back home in an unholy container? When the shaking comes and God's Presence seems like it is about to leave, will they try to steady or prop up the Presence with the "assisting hand of man"? It's a deadly combination.

The moment Uzzah fell to the ground, all the music stopped and an eerie silence settled over the land. Nobody wanted to dance anymore. Nobody wanted to play instruments or to shout and rejoice anymore. What started so well with fanfare and delight had now ended in terrifying death. Have you ever crossed the shaky surface of Nachon's threshing floor in your own life? Do you know what it is like to have things going so well for you one moment, but in a split second after you make a move of presumption, the sky falls in on you?

Earlier in the book I told you that Lois and I lost our son, Matthew, when he was born stillborn after a healthy nine-month pregnancy. Now I need to tell you a little more about our Nachon's threshing floor. Lois and I had already been blessed with two beautiful girls, Debbie and Joanne, but in 1985 we decided to extend our family and we made plans for the event. Lois became pregnant and carried little Matthew nine full months, but the night came when Lois woke me up and said, "We need to go to the hospital. It's started."

As soon as Lois got out of bed, she started to hemorrhage so badly that I had to call for an ambulance. We reached the hospital and Lois went through the labor process, but then the consultant moved me out of the room and talked privately to my wife, and then to me. He said, "Mr. Gott, I'm sorry to tell you this, but your baby has just died."

I went in to see Lois and I took hold of her hand. "Lois, this is probably going to be the toughest couple of hours of our whole lives," I said, "but we'll get through it. Then we'll just have to try and adjust." I was referring to the ordeal Lois still faced. She would have to deliver our baby as if everything was normal, but at the end of her labor, there would be no joy for either of us.

When little Matthew was born, he was perfect in every respect except one. The placenta had broken away and he had died of suffocation because his oxygen supply had been cut off. That was the only reason he died. He wasn't disabled in any way; he was perfect in every way. He looked just like my youngest girl at her birth.

When Matthew was finally delivered, the attendants held him up for me to see. When I saw that he was a boy, I just collapsed to the floor in grief and sadness. Then everyone went into a panic because not only had a beautiful baby boy been delivered stillborn, but Lois began hemorrhaging so rapidly that she nearly died on the delivery table right in front of me. No matter what the doctors did, they couldn't stem the flow of blood. Attendants were desperately squeezing blood transfusion bags in hopes of speeding the blood replacement into her body to save her life. At some point I was pushed out of the room into the corridor, and left alone with my overwhelming anger at God.

My Threshing Floor Experience

I think I know how David felt that day at Nachon's threshing floor. He wasn't so much angry as he was frustrated. In my grief, I was thinking, *God, everything was going so well. The celebration party was in full swing, and now my baby boy has died and my wife is dying in there!* Finally I said out loud, "God, I don't know why the baby died, but I don't know if I could cope if Lois died right now...God, do a miracle. Just do a miracle."

The crash team worked over Lois at a feverish pace, and somehow, in some way known only to God, they managed to pull her through. My wife is alive, but her threshing floor experience permanently marked her. Lois isn't fully recovered even today, more than ten years after Matthew's death. She's right there alongside me in the ministry, and she travels the world with me. We're partners in the Kingdom of God, and I feel like half a man when she's not with me. But Lois hasn't ever reached the 100 percent mark with her health. Her wrestling match with death left her with a limp, if you like, but it keeps us dependent upon God. Every time we get on an airplane, and every time we travel, we have a precious group of intercessors who cover us in prayer around the clock. They carry our moment-by-moment itinerary everywhere with them so every detail of our travels will be bathed in intercessory prayer. We've learned that prayer makes the difference.

When your Nachon's threshing floor comes, it will test who you are, what you are, and what you are carrying. It will shake you and sift your motives, your attitudes, your character, your integrity, and virtually everything else in your life. The threshing floor will strip you bare of every dependency upon the flesh. It will strip you down until it is just "raw God" and nothing else.

The music of celebration and excitement stops at times like that. When lightning strikes at Nachon's place, it's like there is no dancing anymore. There's no more singing or playing of instruments. There's no more rejoicing. Instead you hear people crying out between their moans and shrieks of grief, "God, what do we do? What do we do?!"

Here is the problem: *David still wanted the Presence*, but when he became professional in what he was doing, he began to think that he knew better than God how things should happen and what should take place. It is difficult to understand why Matthew died before he ever saw the light of day, and it is difficult to understand why it happened to a pastor and his wife who had only been in the ministry for a year. But I've learned that God is God and I'm not. I look back on that day in the delivery room and I say, "God, it was horrible when it happened, but I thank You for the things that experience has built into my life, and for what it has done for Lois and I as a couple. You made this thing that the enemy meant for evil into something for our good" (see Gen. 50:20).

Take Me Back to the Shepherd's Field

Are you standing on your own Nachon's threshing floor today? Has your celebration party and ascent to the place you've been waiting for been suddenly stopped by tragedy or confrontation? Has your future evaporated in front of your eyes?

I want to take you back to the shepherd's field, the place where David was nothing but an amateur. In the shepherd's field, he didn't know how to be a king. He didn't know what it was to tell people, "Do this, go here, bring me this!" and see them hurry to obey. All he knew in the shepherd's field was that he could feel the heat from the sun above his head, or gaze at the innumerable stars in the night sky. Accompanied only by the sheep his father had entrusted to his care, David would strip off his outer garments all the way down to a linen ephod, and then he would dance before the Lord with all his might. He would rejoice and sing songs to the Lord and worship Him. Best of all, the shepherd boy David would feel the presence of Jehovah God. Young David felt God as an amateur. He was a man who knew nothing else beyond the boundaries of his shepherd's field except how to worship out of a heart of pure love for God.

Then they made the shepherd boy a king and his heart began to change. Something terrible happened to the man of whom God said, "I have found David the son of Jesse, a man after My own heart, who will do all My will" (Acts 13:22b). When he accepted man's crown, David found he wasn't an amateur anymore. Slowly the poison of pride and arrogance began to creep in as the king became accustomed to saying to his servants, "I know best."

Professionals often feel that they don't need to read God's Book. David the king was in a hurry to get God's ark into his royal city. He was too busy to consult the Book, so he made a professional decision to put the ark of the covenant on a new cart where it would be honored and could be transported faster over the nine-mile stretch to Jerusalem. Then the scene suddenly changed. The cart was shaken and another professional man, a priest, was dead. Everything had stopped and people were standing around in stunned silence. David couldn't just leave the ark there, so he stood in front of his 30,000 hand-picked warriors to ask them a great favor...but as he looked toward them, they turned their faces away. They already knew what the king was going to ask them: "Who wants the ark?"

Who would want the ark when everyone there had just seen it kill somebody? (Even the professional king didn't want it.) The body of the dead man was probably still lying there on the ground when King David stood before them all and said, "We can't leave it here. Who wants it?" Despite everything that had happened, the ark of the covenant was still *the place where men could find the Presence of God.* That is why someone began to push his way through the mighty men.

No Matter the Cost

I can see the scene shifting to blend twentieth century reality with events in the tenth century B.C. A man approached, a little nobody, an amateur no one had ever heard of before. He pushed his way through to the front and declared, "*I'll have the ark.*" When asked, "And who are you?" he says, "*John Arnott.*"

"But it's killing people."

"*It doesn't matter.*"

"You'll lose your reputation."

"*Doesn't matter.*"

"You'll lose your dignity."

"*Doesn't matter.*"

"You'll get thrown out."

"*It doesn't matter. I want the Presence of God.*"

Others began to push forward too. They were more "nobodies" that no one had ever heard of. One guy named Wes Campbell showed up calling himself a "brave heart" with his faced painted blue and wearing a kilt like a Scottish warrior of the thirteenth century. He was one of the first to take his place beside John Arnott and say, "I want the Presence." Another guy comes forward. "Who are you?" the king asks. "Che Ane." "Where are you from?" "Pasadena. I want the Presence." Then someone else comes forward, a *really* unknown nobody with a funny accent.

"Who are you?"

"*Ken Gott.*"

"Never heard of you."

"*Exactly, but I want the Presence.*"

"It's unpredictable, it's messy, it's doing stuff that it shouldn't do. Are you sure you want it?"

"*I want the Presence.*"

King David's little nobody was Obed-Edom, a Philistine who was loyal to David. His name actually means "servant of Edom," and the Edomites were descendants of Jacob's brother, Esau. This is another picture of a lowly race of non-professional people, people outside the religious promises and tradition, who are so hungry for God's Presence that they will risk death to get it. Obed-Edom told King David, "Take the ark to my house. I'll take it." So David ordered his men to take the ark to the house of Obed-Edom and leave it there. The Bible tells us that God blessed everything that Obed-Edom put his hand to. He blessed his crops, his herds and flocks, his children, and his finances. Why? He was prepared to take the Presence home to his house—no matter the cost.

When the Spirit of God showed up in the renewal, we didn't have a long track record of anointing. We didn't have the theology, the doctrine, or even the apologetics to explain what was going on. All we knew was that it was God who was walking among us, and we wanted more of Him. We wanted more of His Presence. Once I tasted the Presence of God, I didn't care if I lost everything. I didn't care if people threw me out or if I lost my reputation and dignity. I just wanted the Presence of God in my life. Then I took the Presence back to Sunderland, a little nowhere place that had been host to some small revivals in the past. A few Celtic monks had risked their lives to bring the gospel to the Sunderland area, and they had established some monastic communities there. But nobody knew about Sunderland. It was just a little seaside town on the North Sea, the coldest thing in the world. It has to be, because it links us with Scandinavia. The cold winds blow down on our coastline from Siberia in the winter, so it can be a horrible little place at times.

I took the Presence back home to Sunderland and the Lord began to bless everything I put my hand to. When the Presence of God came to Sunderland in August, 1994, I had 120 people (counting the children). Two years later I had over 1,000 (counting the children), was given without charge the ten-story Crown House tower, three additional church buildings, a vicarage, and 50 apartments to house the homeless in our area.

The Real Test

Little Obed-Edom was so blessed that the news finally reached King David, who was still moping in his kingly house. David may have made a mistake in judgment, but he was no fool. He knew Obed-Edom was being blessed because the Presence of God was lodging in his home. Now David was down and he was nearly out, but he wasn't finished yet. You need to understand something about Nachon's threshing floor: *The real test is getting up. Will you pick yourself up again?* David had to dig into the heart of courage that God gave him in the shepherd's field. He needed to tap that lion-killing, bear-killing, Goliath-killing courage that can only come from God. That seed of divine courage was still there, buried underneath that professional exterior…if he could just dig deep enough.

When David blew it in front of everyone, the whole nation seemed to turn against him overnight. How would you like to lose your reputation through a single act of stupidity in front of every major leader in the nation? You may not be the king of a nation, but king or not, the day will come when God will take you to the threshing floor! Then He's going to watch to see if you will pick yourself up. Why? Because this world deserves a courageous Church.

No one has any respect for a church of hypocrites and fakers. The world deserves a Church that is full of men and women who don't just shake, fall on the floor, and do all kinds of antics inside a church building—it is looking for a people who "manifests" or displays raw courage in the face of the enemy. The victorious Church does a whole lot more than sing hymns about victory—genuine victors in Christ can stand in the name of their God and declare to every dark power and principality: "We've got a job to do in the name of the Most High God. We're here to destroy the work of the enemy—and that's *you*. If you want to come here and fight us, then here we are. The only direction we're moving is over your head, in Jesus' name." God never took the fight out of the renewal. Spiritual warfare didn't just go to the sidelines; it didn't become a fringe doctrine.

During the Olympic Games held in Barcelona in 1992, Derrick Redmond represented the United Kingdom in the 400-meter sprint. Redmond was one of our greatest medal hopes. He trained for years for the Olympics and went to

Barcelona in peak condition. He was expected to return to England carrying a bronze medal at the very least.

He easily won the first round of heats with a blistering pace, and then he went to the starting blocks for the crucial semifinal rounds, only one race away from the final heat and the race of his dreams. Everything that he'd trained and hoped for was bound up in this one race. It would only last a few seconds, but everything he had accomplished as an athlete was on the line.

I watched with millions of other viewers around the world as Redmond settled into the starting blocks and exploded at the sound of the starter's gun. As soon as he rounded the first curve, Redmon was neck and neck with the leaders. By the time he had reached the second curve he was gradually pulling ahead. On his approach to the third curve, disaster struck. Suddenly Derrick pulls on the back of his thigh and crumples down to the track with a strained hamstring, the most feared injury among sprinters around the world.

The world's TV cameras left Derrick alone on the track—the viewers were only interested in the winners, not the losers. Only after the winners were declared did the TV cameras finally point down the deserted track to the horrifying scene of Derrick Redmond struggling to his feet with his leg dangling uselessly, his face showing the pain of his injury. He focused his eyes on the distant finish line and step by painful step, began to drag his injured leg behind him as he slowly advanced toward the line. Everything that he lived for, the sum of his character and determination, was to pass that finish line, no matter what it cost. His coach ran onto the track and begged Redmond to stop, but he wouldn't listen. Millions of voices around the world whispered or shouted to their TV sets, "You don't have to do this! It could happen to anyone. Runners are always pulling their hamstrings—it was an accident. Don't do this."

Then I saw something that I will never forget. An older man climbed out of the grandstand and began to push his way through the crowd of coaches, security people, and race officials. His eyes were as focused as Derrick Redmond's—he was determined to reach the lone runner struggling to stay on his feet. When this man finally reached Redmond, he put his arm around the runner and took the weight off of the injured leg. Then together these two men walked to the finish line to the thunderous applause of the crowd watching this spectacle. The old man was Derrick Redmond's father. He had to do something when he saw his son draw on every ounce of courage he could muster to *pull himself back up* from disastrous defeat and serious injury so he could *finish the race that he had begun.*

The Second Time Around

That is a picture of what our heavenly Father is waiting to do when we get flattened and devastated by the threshing floor of Nachon. If He sees us try to get back up after a devastating fall, if He sees us draw on every ounce of courage we have as we do what we can with our strained abilities and strengths, then He will come out of the grandstand of Heaven and help us reach our destiny beyond the finish line. We might have a limp, but then we have to lean just a little bit harder on our Father when He comes to help us.

The Church needs to be a prophetic, radical, courageous Church that is determined to get up again after every adversity or heavy blow. David picked himself up after three months had passed and decided it was time to go for the ark again. But this time he read the Book of God to see what

God says about transporting the ark of the covenant. He discovered that he needed to assign Levite priests to the task, and they were to carefully carry the ark on two long poles run through loops on the ark.

In "Act Two" of the return of the ark, David came out with all the singers and musicians for another try. The new cart was burnt, and the priests, the descendants of Levi, were commanded to carry the ark of the covenant. This time, David told the Levites and the sons of Aaron, "Put it on your shoulder this time around. It will be all right—I've read the Book." David wasn't in a hurry on the second attempt. He had the priests offer sacrifices and the people worshiped and praised God throughout the trip to Jerusalem.

It takes faith to carry the Presence of God. You may not feel it at all times, but you've got to believe, *I'm a carrier of the Presence.* According to God's Word, the Presence of His glory sits nowhere better than on the shoulders of the priesthood—people like you and I. Once the priests had passed through the crucial process of shouldering the weight of the ark (without being struck dead), the intensity of the celebration grows with every step toward Jerusalem. Finally David does something very unusual by "professional" standards. The Bible says he stripped off everything that was symbolic of his kingship. He removed his crown, his sandals, and his royal robes, and he even left his chariot behind. The King of Israel and Judah suddenly stripped down to his shepherd-boy clothes. He reverted to type as the boy who was content to be a shepherd boy, a mere amateur in the field, just worshiping God in the cool of the day. Once again David the king had become David the worshiper, the shepherd who knew nothing else but how to love and please God. The professional had become an amateur again.

David began to dance before the Lord with all his might. He worshiped God with total abandonment to the opinions of men and angels. He wasn't bothered about what people thought about his reputation and kingly dignity. All he knew was, "There was a time when I used to do this every day! Oh, it feels so good to be doing it again!" Yes!

Let me apply this to our lives today. Do you remember the day when you were born again? You were face to face with "raw God" and nothing and no one else. Do you remember how clean you felt? Do you remember how joyful you felt, and how God's peace just flooded your soul? You used to sing to God and worship Him constantly, and you had to tell everybody about Jesus! In the beginning, you were nothing but a happy amateur in the field. What happened? You got professional. People told you to settle down and bring yourself under control, and you did.

You know what you need to do, don't you. It is time to spiritually strip down to your linen ephod. You need to feel the joy of being an anointed amateur in the field once again—with all the uninhibited dancing, singing, praise, and boldness you had for your first love, Jesus. It really feels good. Revert to type—go back to your first love, to the simple love and passion of your life as an anointed amateur in the field.

Chapter 8

Treating a Lazy Eye

There was another professional in David's life. She was the one peeking through a window as David danced before the Lord. She was also the professional who sneered and despised him for it. She was Michal, David's first wife and the youngest daughter of King Saul. In other words, she was a professional royal family member.

All of Israel (outside the royal chambers) celebrated the night that the ark of the covenant was carried into Jerusalem on the shoulders of the Levites. David personally led the people in unrestrained, uninhibited worship and praise before God, and he distributed gifts of food and drink to the people and instructed the priests to offer sacrifices to God. Then he returned home to bless his household. That is when he was confronted by his wife, Michal.

Several years earlier, King Saul had taken Michal away from David when his son-in-law fled for his life. The king gave Michal to another man named Palti to become Palti's wife just to spite David (see 1 Sam. 25:44). Michal was finally returned to David by Ishbosheth (one of Saul's sons) after Saul's death and just before David's victory over the Philistines and the return of the ark. Michal grew up in King Saul's court, and after being wrenched from the surroundings of the royal court for so many years, she was glad to be "a royal" again (even if she wasn't so pleased to be back with David). Her first concern seemed to be the continuation of her royal rights and privileges as a wife of the king rather than pleasing God.

> *Then David returned to bless his household. And Michal the daughter of Saul came out to meet David, and said, "How glorious was the king of Israel today, uncovering himself today in the eyes of the maids of his servants, as one of the base fellows shamelessly uncovers himself!" So David said to Michal, "It was before the Lord, who chose me instead of your father and all his house, to appoint me ruler over the people of the Lord, over Israel. Therefore I will play music before the Lord. And **I will be even more undignified than this**, and will be humble in my own sight. But as for the maidservants of whom you have spoken, by them I will be held in honor." Therefore Michal the daughter of Saul had no children to the day of her death (2 Samuel 6:20-23).*

Michal thought she knew how a king should behave. After all, didn't she grow up in a king's household? She remembered the ways the common people used to respond to her father. She watched them bow to him, praise him, and beg him for mercy. She remembered that when he snapped his fingers, the military leaders and palace servants literally ran to follow his every command. She felt that any reproach on David was a reproach on her and her status as a queen.

She told her husband, "You shamed yourself today when you stripped down and danced around in front of all those women. You sure didn't look like a king!" David's answer to his jealous and self-centered wife is being echoed around today: "I wasn't dancing for you or anyone else on this earth! I was dancing before Him who knew me when I was a nobody. I was dancing for the One who called me when I was nothing, who knew me when I was only a shepherd in a field. I'm dancing for the God who made me, an anointed amateur, the king of Israel. And if it is necessary, I will be *even more undignified than this....*"

It's Not Going to Get Any Better

Today, thousands of modern Davids explain their uninhibited joy in the Presence of God by saying, "I'm not dancing and shouting for you or anyone else on earth. I'm rejoicing in front of Him who saw me and chose me when I was a drug addict, when I was losing my life. I'm dancing and twirling for joy before Him who loved me when I was an alcoholic in the gutter. I'm dancing before the One who saw me when I had no life at all, the One who called me into His Kingdom in spite of my weaknesses. And if necessary, *I'll get worse!* So listen: *It is not going to get any better!*"

Michal thought that she knew how a king should behave (and she did), but she had no idea how a shepherd boy in a field behaves! That was the problem. David wasn't a king that day. He had reverted back to type; he was a shepherd boy in a field, dancing before the Lord with all his might. We've got the same communication problem today when people come up to us and say, "Oh, you are a disgrace. You don't even know how to behave in church." (*That's the truth if ever I heard it!*) "You don't know how to behave with decent, respectable, church-going people." I have to say that's true, because I'm *not* one of them. I've lost the ability to distinguish whether I'm in church or out of church—all I know is that I'm standing before God. I'm rejoicing before the One I love more than anything or anyone else. It's because of Him that I'm like this! (And I'm not going to get any better!)

The man-pleasing disease that destroyed Saul tainted everything his family did. First of all, Michal's father, King Saul, tried to make an anointed amateur from the fields fight Goliath with the useless weapons and armor of a rejected professional. Many years later in Jerusalem, Michal herself was criticizing David, the anointed amateur in the field, because he couldn't fit into the kingly professional mold of her father, Saul—even though God had clearly rejected Saul's professional man-pleasing ways. The power behind David's leadership anointing from the field was too powerful to be contained in the old flesh-based equipment and "wineskins" of Saul's professional reign. Years later, Jesus told His disciples that you don't put new wine into old wineskins—the explosive, expansive power in the new wine is too powerful and volatile for the old, cracked, inflexible wineskins of the past (see Mt. 9:17).

How does this apply to the current move of God in renewal and revival? If you haven't noticed, there are a lot of people (let's call them "professionals") who have some very strong ideas about how you should behave in church. They are quick to tell you and anyone else who will listen, "Our generation of believers has been around for a long time, and frankly, these new people who are coming in and getting touched by God just aren't doing it right! They are not behaving properly. I've seen them shout out at the wrong times, and I've even seen them fall off their chairs right in the middle of services—and everybody knows that chairs are made to be sat upon. These people laugh out loud when there is nothing to laugh at, and they keep getting excited when there is nothing to be excited about."

The worst offense of all seems to be the fact that "these people" just won't keep quiet and do things the way they should be done. When they are told to be quiet or to stop dancing, they may say the same thing David told Michal. I've heard people say, "When is all this going to stop?" *Never.* This is not a phase we are going through. This is not something that is going to come and go. I've even heard some professionals tell one another, "It's over." That is wishful thinking. Perhaps if they say it enough times they will convince a few people who have never danced as an anointed amateur in the field, but it won't work for anyone who has felt the hand of God on his or her life. Once God visits you in the field, you can't be convinced by words. You have experienced something that has changed your life forever.

If you have experienced the touch of God's glory in this move of God, then you have probably heard one or more versions of these comments: "Oh, I remember a time when you used to sit in church like a sensible person. I remember a time when you used to sit in church quietly, and you did all the right things at the right moment. Yes, you've disgraced yourself now by joining that renewal bunch and the revival crowd. Frankly, you're a disgrace. I can't even bring my family members to church any more. I don't dare! I can't let them see you like this." I counsel you to tell them what David told Michal:

> "Well, I've got news for you: *This is not going to get any better. I'm just going to get worse!* Oh, if the Lord wants me to shake for ten hours, then let the shaking begin! If I've got to lie on the carpet for three days, then for goodness' sake, Lord, put me on the carpet! I'm not

doing this just to impress you and make you angry. I'm doing this for the God who knew me when I was a nobody from nowhere. Nobody knew where Sunderland was or who Ken Gott was. But God looked into my heart and stepped into my life to pick me up. He took me by the arm and said, 'Come on, we'll walk together, you and I.' It's before Him that I'm a disgrace. It's before Him that I become totally abandoned to His praise and glory. Don't you see—it is for Him alone, and no one else. And I'm not going to get any better. I'm just going to get worse."

The Bible tells us that Michal became barren the moment she criticized David for worshiping God like an anointed amateur in the field (see 2 Sam. 6:23). That is a frightening statement. That meant God was listening in on their private conversation, and He held Michal personally accountable for aiming her scoffing words at His anointed amateur.

We need to be careful not to become barren and unfruitful, as we gaze out of the windows of our "palaces" of professionalism, because we despise in our hearts those things that we may not understand. I often think, *Oh God. I never want to despise anything in my heart. I never want to be barren; I want to be fruitful in everything that I put my hand to. I want the Presence, and I want more of it. I want God to put it here on my shoulders, and I want to be a carrier of His Presence.* The Bible tells us later on that though Michal never had children, she did raise the five sons of another man from Saul's family line, but even those grown sons were sacrificed to atone for the sins of Saul and to remove famine from the land (see 2 Sam. 21:1-9). Again, death came to Saul's household because Saul the professional had sinned against God by trying to please man rather than by honoring the Word and commands of God.

I feel for those who are saying, "This revival business isn't God. This is not Him. This is not how people should behave." I pray that they will never be barren, but it is too late to convince me that they are right. I've been around the world, and I've seen the fires of genuine revival in Pensacola, Argentina, Toronto, and Australia. I've traveled and ministered in North America from coast to coast, and I have to tell you that *this is not going away*.

Recover Your Passion

I love Jesus Christ with all my heart, and I thought I was very passionate about my walk with Him. Then I visited Brownsville Assembly of God in Pensacola, Florida, and I met Pastor John Kilpatrick and Evangelist Stephen Hill. I thought I was passionate until I heard Steve Hill talking about George Whitefield. He said George Whitefield used to preach sometimes so long and so hard during the Great Awakening that his throat bled. Then Steve looked up to God and said, "Oh God, make my throat bleed for You." This evangelist for the revival in that church actually wants to preach so hard and so long that his throat bleeds for Jesus. That's why God's hand is moving in a continuous revival there that is headed toward its third anniversary! The numbers of people born again in that revival are listed in the hundreds of thousands, and the leaders of the revival insist on cutting down every conservative estimate just to make sure they are not guilty of exaggeration. Pensacola was literally the only place I have ever been in an evangelistic service where the evangelist says to the ushers, "Hold them back. I haven't opened the altar yet." People were trying to get to the front before Steve Hill had actually given the appeal, so the ushers had to hold them back to maintain order! I wish more churches around the world would have that problem!

I don't see one reason on earth why the same thing shouldn't happen in England, in Germany, in Japan, in Russia, in Korea, in India, in Belize, in Indonesia, or in Lancaster, California, and Bangor, Maine! People are people and God is God, and those are really the only two ingredients you need: the Savior and those who need to be saved. It hasn't changed in 2,000 years. There is no other formula. God said:

> *And it shall come to pass afterward that I will pour out My Spirit on all flesh; your sons and your daughters shall prophesy, your old men shall dream dreams, your young men shall see visions. And also on My menservants and on My maidservants I will pour out My Spirit in those days (Joel 2:28-29).*

The more flesh upon which God can pour His Spirit on, the more we'll get! Some of you love God with a passion, but you have become too professional, and you've put on some garments that made you "too good for God." Have you crossed any threshing floors lately? Is your man-made ministry and is your man-pleasing success about to be shaken? Have you noticed some things going a little bit awry in your life and ministry? All the Lord wants to do is get your heart turned back to the God of your childhood, to your first love. We are not all prodigals or drug addicts needing deliverance and salvation from a lifestyle of sin. We are not all alcoholics or career criminals—some of us have been in church since the day we were born, yet inside in our hearts *we have drifted away*. Everything looks good on the outside, but the problem is that it's *too good*. God isn't interested in professionals who lean on everything but Him to achieve success in ministry and religion. God is for amateurs, anointed amateurs in the field, who know how to worship Him in spirit and in truth.

Here is a prophetic word for you: Do what David did. Strip off that professional stuff men have given you and rejoice in the Lord with all your might! He will purify you and set you free if you are willing to forget about what the person next to you thinks. Focus your "desire to please" on God, not man. When you stand before Jesus in Heaven, it is you and Him. The person next to you won't be included in that exclusive two-way conversation—that individual will be having his or her own private encounter with the living God.

You know you have heard the voice of God speak to your heart through this chapter if there is something within you that is crying out, "I want passion again! I want to return to the God of my childhood. I need to return to the God I met when I first got saved—I want that God. I want the God who lifted me out of the world and saved my soul. I need to return to those days when He was the passion of my life."

During the second week of the renewal in Sunderland, one of the first ministers from the area to visit us was a staff pastor from the local Open Brethren church, Dr. Philip Le Dune. Philip was a family physician in practice with his father, who was also a physician and the senior minister at their church. He had heard about the strange happenings in our renewal meetings, and he decided to investigate for himself. This is his story:

"I could not actually understand what was going on in the meetings. I could not work out why people were jerking and shaking. In fact, to me it looked like they needed some Valium more than anything else. I thought they were fibbing, you know? I wanted to tell them, 'Look, what is going on here?'

"But even though I couldn't understand it with my mind, something in my heart said, 'This is God.' I'd never been more conscious of the Presence of God before, even though it was completely out of my tradition with the Brethren. I kept going back to the renewal meetings over the next few days, and I kept seeing more and more strange things that I couldn't understand. As a doctor, I was trained to analyze and break everything down. I automatically thought of the worst prognosis. My analytical mind wouldn't really cope with it, and I kept saying to God, 'What is going on here, Lord?'

"Then God showed me a picture one day when I was at work at our family medical clinic. I saw a small boy who had a squint, a lazy eye. I was talking to a friend when God said to me, '*The Church has got a lazy eye, and it's in danger of going blind.*'

"And I knew from my medical training that when you have a lazy eye, the brain will eventually ignore one of the eyes, so it will become blind. It can't cope with the double vision created by the signals from the lazy eye, because one eye will look across at the far wall while the other one will look straight ahead. This forces the brain to decide which eye it's going to rely on. It naturally tends to rely on the eye that's looking straight ahead.

"The treatment for lazy eye is to put a patch over one of the eyes for a time. You don't patch the weak eye as many would suppose. Instead, you patch the strong eye, and that brings the weak eye back into true alignment to compensate for the loss. It is an interesting fact, isn't it? Although the treatment seems simple, the results of ignoring a lazy eye condition is catastrophic—it will result in blindness in one eye.

"So God said to me, 'I am patching the strong eye of the Church. I'm patching the eye of your intellect and understanding, because this is the eye you are relying on, in order to strengthen up the eye of your heart and bring it in line again. The reason you don't *understand* it is because I'm patching it.'

"I began to understand why there were things that I just did not understand at all about what was going on in those renewal meetings. Then God said to me one night when I was lying on the carpet, 'Do you know what a sign and a wonder is?'

"I told Him, 'A sign is something that points somewhere.' Then He asked, 'What about a wonder?'

"I said, 'I don't really know what a wonder is.' Then He said, 'Well, a wonder is *a thing you wonder about*, and that's what you're doing.' I began to feel comfortable at that stage, even though I wasn't able to analyze and understand things with my mind. I remembered the Bible verse that says, 'Trust in the Lord with all your heart, and lean not on your own understanding' " (Prov. 3:5).

Heart and Head Alignment

The Church has relied on its own understanding so much that it has forgotten totally about the eye of the heart. We have prided ourselves on our knowledge and our professional training so much that we lost our shepherd's anointing birthed in intimate relationship with God. We need knowledge, but we don't need the pride that comes with knowledge elevated to the level of an idol. God intends to "patch our eye" only for a season. Once our "heart and relationship eye" gets as strong as our "understanding eye," then God will remove the patch from our understanding. Until then, people will be virtually unable to perceive or understand the supernatural works of God in renewal and revival meetings. God wants to bring depth perception back to the Church. He wants us to enjoy equally good vision in our hearts and our heads. We need stereoscopic vision in the Church.

Dr. Philip Le Dune was able to remove his "patch" very quickly, and today he pastors Gosforth Christian Centre in Newcastle, a thriving outreach church we planted through this ministry. Only God could send me a pastor for the revival from the Open Brethren Church. Philip's father even gave his official blessing and "sent" his son to work with us under Christ. Unity and inter-church cooperation is another conspicuous fruit proving that true renewal and revival is in the land.

Our bookstores and libraries are filled with book after book on methodology, programming, and techniques for church growth. We have acquired great head knowledge on what the Church should be, what it should look like, and how it should act or respond to various situations. The problem is that while we've busied ourselves accumulating our knowledge and our professional wardrobe, we became too good to pay attention to God Himself. We thought we could have church without Him. Like the church of Ephesus visited by the angel in the Book of Revelation, we think we are so good that we are qualified to discern false apostles:

> *To the angel of the church of Ephesus write, "These things says He who holds the seven stars in His right hand, who walks in the midst of the seven golden lampstands: 'I know your works, your labor, your patience, and that you cannot bear those who are evil. And you have tested those who say they are apostles and are not, and have found them liars; and you have persevered and have patience, and have labored for My name's sake and have not become weary.* **Nevertheless I have this against you, that you have left your first love.** *Remember therefore from where you have fallen; repent and do the first works, or else I will come to you quickly and remove your lampstand from its place; unless you repent' " (Revelation 2:1-5).*

Love and passion for the Lord will take you a lot further than head knowledge. If we get too puffed up with knowledge divorced from passion, we'll become professionals who don't know God. We'll end up losing one of our eyes. The Lord is pulling our lazy eye back into alignment. We're beginning to use relationship words like *intimacy* and *passion* again, because we are returning to our first love. One universal fruit of renewal and revival services around the world is the rebirth of passionate, all-out love for Jesus Christ. Pastor Cleddie Keith of Kentucky said in one of our revival meetings, "One thing this move of God is doing is making amateurs of us all." Praise God!

We need to yield to the treatment of the Great Physician. For a season, we must submit to His "patch" and lay down our negative, doubting intellects and submit to His baptism of fire and passion. He wants to strip away all our professional costumes, credentials, and crowns so we can worship, dance, and cavort before Him like joyful children once again. God is for amateurs, not professionals.

Amateurs know they need help, but professionals are constantly tempted to write their own book and go their own way. Amateurs know their credentials are faulty at best, but professionals think that they actually deserve to be worshiped for their knowledge and ability. Many of us aren't quite prepared to become amateurs yet, but our hunger for the freedom of the field is growing moment by moment, and our hearts are about to burst out of our bulky professional costumes. Praise God, our condition isn't going to get any better. It's just going to get worse! God is determined to bring His Church back into alignment.

Chapter 9

Arrested

I press on, that I may lay hold of that for which Christ Jesus has also laid hold of me (Philippians 3:12b).

Paul wanted to lay hold of or arrest the things of God in the same way Jesus Christ arrested him. Notice that there are two "arresters" and two "arrestees" in this verse. First God *arrested* the man He had chosen. Then the chosen man *arrested* the call, the purpose, and the anointing that God had for him.

God didn't arrest Paul by lightly catching his clothing and saying, "Listen, I don't know if you're aware of it, but you're actually going to burn in hell. Now if you would like, I can explain My redemption plan, or you can just go your own way." No, Jesus knocked Paul off of his high horse and blinded him until he saw the light with his heart.

When you've been knocked to the ground and blinded for three days, when your face has been ground into the dust, you know you've been *arrested*. Paul knew what it was to lay hold of that for which Christ Jesus laid hold of him.

The Bible says, "The kingdom of heaven suffers violence, and the violent take it by force" (Mt. 11:12b). In other words, they take it and make it theirs. I want to lay hold, arrest, and apprehend that for which Christ Jesus took hold of me.

As a 17-year-old youth, I got arrested by God. I didn't feel a little tug on my jacket; I felt His powerful arm pull my arm up behind my back, and I felt another massive arm encircle my chest and tighten around my neck. I heard His authoritative voice say to my heart, "You're busted. You are under arrest, Ken Gott. From now on, you are going where I am going."

Before I entered the ministry, I used to be a Bobby, or a policeman. Since a policeman is charged with keeping the peace and enforcing the laws, then every law enforcement officer has to know how to arrest people. If I saw a man put his foot through the plate-glass window of a department store and setting off all the burglar alarms, then I would have to take some action.

What if I walked up to this man and took a light hold on his shirt sleeve with my thumb and first finger before saying, "Excuse me, sir. That was very naughty. I don't know if you're aware of this, but actually you're not allowed to kick in windows like that. Now I'll give you the benefit of a doubt and assume that you probably didn't realize you weren't supposed to put your foot through this window. Now why don't we go down to the police office and fill out a few forms. After that I'll just put you in a jail cell until your sister can get you out. Then you will stand in front of the judge, get sentenced to prison or pay a fine, and everything will be taken care of. What do you say?"

Has this man been arrested? Does he realize that he has been caught and there is no choice but to submit and reap the consequences of his deed? No, I haven't communicated any of that at all. I've given him a lot of contradictory words, and my "grip" on him invites defiance and escape. All he has to do is shrug his shoulder and he can escape arrest. That's why you never see police officers making arrests like that.

I was trained to effect an arrest by communicating my authority with physical pressure as well as with my words. First I would quickly grab one of the suspect's hands and twist it behind his back. This wasn't a gentle movement—it was done with power and authority. That gives the suspect a clear, unmistakable message. When my other arm goes across his chest and tightens around his neck, he knows the days of freedom are over. From that moment on, that person will be going where I am going—whether he wants to or not. That is what the apostle Paul was talking about in his letter to the Philippians. "I've laid hold, I've arrested and apprehended you. I've arrested and apprehended the thing you have for me."

God has apprehended this generation for a very specific reason that is described throughout the Bible. The Book of Revelation speaks of it as "a pure river of water of life, clear as crystal, proceeding from the throne of God and of the Lamb" (Rev. 22:1). God invites us to come to His river in the New Testament, while in the Old Testament the prophets said, "*Go to* the river." The difference is that Jesus Christ Himself *is* the river of God.

Only Jesus in all creation can rightly say, "Come to Me, all you who labor and are heavy laden, and I will give you rest" (Mt. 11:28). It is Jesus Christ who said, "But whosoever drinketh of the water that I shall give him shall never thirst; but the water that I shall give him shall be in him a well of water springing up into everlasting life" (Jn. 4:14 KJV). It was Jesus who stood up in crowded Jerusalem on the holiest feast day of Israel and shouted, "...If anyone thirsts, let him come to Me and drink. He who believes in Me, as the Scripture has said, out of his heart will flow rivers of living water" (Jn. 7:37-38). The Psalmist wrote, "There is a river whose streams shall make glad the city of God, the holy place of the tabernacle of the Most High. God is in the midst of her, she shall not be moved..." (Ps. 46:4-5).

The Church is in the same place as the school of the prophets under Elisha. We have already been arrested by God and called to the river. Now it is up to us to arrest or apprehend God's anointing and purpose. Unfortunately, many of us have spent decades working to build our house with borrowed tools and borrowed anointing, and now all seems lost in the river. We need a miracle, and we need courage to act when God says act.

A Borrowed Anointing

And the sons of the prophets said to Elisha, "See now, the place where we dwell with you is too small for us. Please, let us go to the [River] Jordan, and let every man take a beam from there, and let us make there a place where we may dwell." So he answered, "Go." Then one said, "Please consent to go with your servants." And he answered, "I will go." So he went with them. And when they came to the Jordan, they cut down trees. But as one was cutting down a tree, the iron ax head fell into the water; and he cried out and said, "Alas, master! For it was borrowed." So the man of God said, "Where did it fall?" And he showed him the place. So he cut off a stick, and threw it in there; and he made the iron float. Therefore he said, "Pick it up for your-self." So he reached out his hand and took it (2 Kings 6:1-7).

Do you know why the axe head fell off in the first place? It is probably because it was blunt, and the reason it was blunt could have been because it was *borrowed*. The problem with borrowed things is that you never look after them quite like you look after your own things. Isn't that true? Think about it. When did your neighbor ever return your tool in the same shape as when he borrowed it from you? He didn't look after it like you would have, did he? Did your wrenches come back smeared with oil? Was the edge of your hammer nicked? Did that chisel came back with a few pieces chipped off the edges? (It's probably the same when you borrow his tools too.)

This has an important application to the ministry as well. You can't borrow another man's anointing. You can't take your pastor's anointing and make it yours. You can't take the anointing that is upon me and say, "I'll have that." Yes, there is such a thing as impartation, and I preach and practice that constantly. But the only source of true anointing is God, and God never gives anointing without requiring some investment on our part.

What you need is your own anointing from God. His anointing is abundant, and He delights in giving abundantly to all who want to operate and work in the power of the Holy Spirit. Honestly, there's enough of God's anointing to go around for every one of us. You don't need to borrow. Don't look at an anointed musician and say, "Oh, I want his anointing." Don't look at someone on the prayer team and say, "Oh, I wish I had her anointing." Don't look at so-called giants in God and say, "Oh, I want their anointing." How about *your* anointing? How about the anointing *that God wants to give you*? Are you willing to pay the price to apprehend and arrest it?

If you borrow an anointing, if you coast along on the faith and labor of another man, then eventually you'll not look after it like your own. If you borrow an axe head from another man to build your own house, you probably won't invest the time and effort it takes to sharpen it, oil it, and keep it clean after each use. In the end, you'll be in the same place as the sons of the prophets. You'll end up trying to cut down trees with a dead stick in your hand, because the borrowed axe head will just fly away into the river. Your cutting edge will be gone. At first, your borrowed anointing will help you cut down a few trees and make a little progress on your house. You could pretend that you had your own anointing, and you can manipulate it and make it work for you for awhile. But the more you use it, the more ineffective and dull it will become until finally you are swinging your axe so hard that the borrowed anointing will fly, leaving you holding a dry and dead stick in your hand.

How can you know if you are one of the people who have tried to build their houses on borrowed anointing? The symptoms are pretty obvious. Are you crying out in your heart, "God, I'm just burned out. I'm tired and worn out. I'm just too weary to go on anymore." The problem might be that you are trying to cut down trees with a dead stick. Day after day, you are just hitting trees with a dead stick and trying to make it work. You are trying to clear a space and make a place to hold a bigger anointing, but you're doing it with borrowed anointing and hitting living trees with a dead stick. The cutting edge is gone from your life and ministry. It is lost in the river and you don't know how to retrieve it because it would take a miracle. Worst of all, you know that no matter how hard you try, a dead stick can't chop down trees.

Retrieve Your Anointing

There is a solution, but don't bother to try it unless you've determined in your heart that you don't want anybody else's anointing! The cure to your problem will cost you something. I love the anointing and I love being around anointed people. I love it when anointed people speak words of life into my heart and spirit. I love being around the healing anointing and the anointing of deliverance. There is no substitute for the anointing of God, but it only comes from one source, and that Source is a river—a moving, living river that challenges us to act by faith.

I am writing this book under a strong anointing, and this message was given to me by God through the anointing He gave me. That's not a boast or an arrogant statement; it's just a fact. I have no power or special ability in and of myself. I write, preach, minister, and serve under an anointing that God gave to me. In the beginning, I used to desire the gifts I saw in anointed men and women. Now I focus my desire on the Giver of the gifts. Paul told us in First Corinthians that we should desire the best gifts, but he made it clear where those gifts come from (see 1 Cor. 12).

I've made up my mind that I want to know God. The cutting edge that I have is mine. God invested His anointing in me, and He expects me to treat it respectfully and carefully, as if it were my own. It isn't another man's, and it isn't borrowed. Because I know it's mine, I'll keep it sharp. I'll exercise it every day. I'll move in it and oil it every day. I'll do everything that I need to do to keep this anointing sharp. Why? Because it's not borrowed, it's not somebody else's, it is the anointing that God gave Ken Gott. It is a "talent" He gave to me, and He holds me responsible for investing and caring for that talent so it will produce dividends. I am using my anointing from God to clear a space and make a bigger place for God to dwell in my life. I'm not hitting trees with a dead stick anymore. Something is happening because there's an edge to my life and ministry that God gave to me. And I want that anointing to increase.

God wants to take the weariness out of your life this very moment if you have been struggling along on borrowed anointing (I'm talking as a pastor now). He wants to take away that weariness and striving. He wants to put an edge to your life that you've lost in the river or never had in the first place. (The moment you started to envy someone else's gift, you let your borrowed axe head fall. The moment you wanted to be like someone else, your axe head fell.)

How do you retrieve a blunt, borrowed, iron axe head from a flowing river? It takes a miracle, because iron doesn't float. Scientists don't like us saying it, but the anointing can do anything in the hands of our big God! The anointing can even make iron float.

So the man of God said, "Where did it fall?" And he showed him the place. So he cut off a stick, and threw it in there; and he made the iron float. Therefore he said, "Pick it up for yourself." So he reached out his hand and took it (2 Kings 6:6-7).

Jesus Christ is asking every one of us who feels weary and worn, "Where did you lose it? Where did it fall? Where did you drop it, and what happened to your heart?"

Where did you lose it? Come on, track back just a little bit. Where did it fall? Well, the good thing is, iron does float, and we serve the God of the second chance, and the third chance, and the fourth, and the fifth, and the sixth chance. In fact, we serve a God who will come and pursue us time, and time, and time again.

When the prodigal came to himself, he returned to the father's heart, to the father's house. The only time in Scripture we see God running to anybody, He's running to a returning prodigal. The Bible says that before the prodigal saw the father, the father had seen the prodigal, and before the prodigal could run to the father, the father was already running to the prodigal. He put his arms around him and declared, "He who was lost is now found, and he who was dead is now alive." (See Luke 15:11-24.)

God hasn't changed. He'll run to you when you've declared the place where you've lost it. When you've repented of it, the Father will run to you. And by the power of the Spirit, He'll make the iron float. Don't ever say, "My circumstances are too difficult for God." Don't ever say, "My circumstances are so complex, God can't unravel them." My big God makes iron float, and my big God shall provide for all your needs according to His riches in glory (see Phil. 4:19). This God makes iron float!

A New and Living Stick

David knew what it was like to lose the anointing. He knew what it was like to be left high and dry right beside the river with a dead stick in his hand. David was known as the man after God's own heart, and the man who would do anything that God asked him to do. He earned that reputation when he was nothing but an anointed amateur. He was nothing but an anointed amateur when he killed the lion and the bear, and he was an anointed amateur when he killed Goliath the giant.

Once David turned professional and began to operate with a borrowed anointing, something happened to his heart. Once they put man's robe of recognition on him, once they crowned him as a power unto himself, once they put rings on him and put him in a king's chariot, he left his own amateur's anointing behind and took up a borrowed anointing from adoring people. He looked every part the king, but something happened to his heart and he lost the edge.

If Goliath had come along at that point, I doubt if David could have done anything about it. The "borrowed Saul anointing" wouldn't have fazed the giant. If the lion and the bear had attacked the sheep, I doubt if David could have done anything about it—they think nothing of dead sticks in the hands of costumed pretenders. When David relied on his blunted, borrowed anointing to bring home the anointing of God in the ark of the covenant, his borrowed axe head flew off into the river and he was left holding the dead stick of failure and disgrace in his hands. Somewhere between the shepherd's field and the throne of Israel, David lost his own cutting edge, and the borrowed anointing he was using fell and was lost. And he didn't even know that he had lost his own edge.

Like the prophet of God, Jesus is asking us today, "Where did you lose it? Where did it fall?" Our answer is predictable but acceptable: "God, I repent. I got caught up in this and I got caught up in that. I tried to do it this way and it didn't work. Then I tried to do it that way with a borrowed anointing. Now I'm weary and worn out from hitting trees with a dead stick. God, that's where it fell. I repent." Thank God the story doesn't end there. We serve a miracle-working God who loves to perform the impossible on our behalf. When the man showed Elisha where the axe head had fallen, the prophet cut a new stick and threw it into the river, making the iron axe head float (see 2 Kings 6:6).

God wants to give you a new stick, but first you need to throw away the stick that you've been hitting trees with. It's good for nothing. Now, God isn't going to give you just any stick. He has cut a new stick for you from the Living Vine. It is alive, not dead. It pulsates with the life and miracle-working power of God. It bears fruit in its season; its leaf never withers (see Ps. 1:3). This stick will bud in your hand and produce fruit even as you watch it (see Num. 17:8). Why? It has been cut from the Vine Himself. Let God throw His living Branch over the place where you lost your edge!

Do you know what God will say at that point? He'll say the same thing Elisha said to his pupil: *"Pick it up for yourself."* Can you believe it? "Pastor, I'm in a spot of bother, can you help me?" "Pick it up for yourself." "House group leader, I need you to help me with my problem." "Pick it up for yourself."

There is a good chance that you don't like this point because I just wiped out the pastoral ministry of the church and gave every worn-out pastor a new line. Yes! If God performs the miracle, if God makes the iron float, why do you want the pastor to pick it up? If God has done it, *pick it up for yourself*!

Now I want to tell you something very profound. The living Branch wasn't thrown into a reservoir, lake, or pond. No, the prophet threw that stick into a *river*! One of the characteristics of a river is that it *moves*. That water was not standing still. It wouldn't wait for the man to wait or debate, and it isn't going to wait around today for you to think about it. By the time some of us skeptical critics finally pick up God's stick, our cutting edge has floated down the river

20 yards or more! If God says, "Pick it up," then pick it up now! Lay hold of God's Branch—arrest your destiny or lose it. You're dealing with a flowing river on the move. If you really want the anointing for your life, if you really want your edge back, then you will have to run for it! You may even have to plunge into the river to retrieve your edge.

When that iron floats, my friend, it isn't time to hang around and discuss the options. You have none. Pursue it or lose it. Take hold of your miracle and acknowledge that it is God's gift to *you*. He made that anointing float to the surface of the river for you and your situation. Like the apostle Paul before you, you are to "lay hold of that for which Christ Jesus laid hold of you." I don't know about you, but I'm a man who has been apprehended and arrested by God, and now it's my turn to get a grip on my destiny and anointing and never let go.

Make Room for the New

Several years ago, before the "Father's Blessing" came to Toronto, John and Carol Arnott traveled to Buenos Aires, Argentina, and received prayer from a wonderful friend, Claudio Freidzon. Claudio is a mighty man of the Spirit who had experienced a great outpouring of God's anointing in a revival that was sweeping across his nation. When he prayed for John Arnott, he slapped John's hands and said, "Take it!" For the first time in his life, John Arnott thought, *You know, I think I will. Lord, whatever it was You put there, I'm taking it.* And he did.

The iron floated for John and Carol Arnott down in Argentina, and they took it. That was the axe head floating for the "Toronto Blessing," and John took hold of it. The rest is history and a drama of God's outpouring that is still expanding and growing.

God wants that iron to float in your life too. My "iron" floated to the surface of the river in August of 1994, when Lois and I went to Toronto. When I saw that iron floating to the top, I took hold of it. I didn't know it at the time, but that cutting edge of anointing was for the Sunderland Refreshing and for all that God has done since then! When that iron floated up in that little airport church in Canada, I took hold of that for which Christ Jesus took hold of me.

There's a degree of violence about this. This is not a picture of a meek and mild Jesus coming to us. This is Jesus the Kings of kings and Lord of lords coming as a warrior and as our Commander in Chief. This is a picture of a supreme commander mobilizing a mighty army of men and women who dare to rise up and take hold of their destiny in Jesus!

The iron in your life is going to float up with a new edge, a new anointing. If you ask God to throw His Branch over the place where you dropped your anointing, then He will cause a new anointing to float to the top of His river today. First you must admit that you've lost your edge or that you've been struggling along on borrowed anointing. Then be willing to throw down your dead stick so you can take hold of your new anointing once God floats it again.

You may be in the front line ministry described in Ephesians 4. You may be serving in an "ascension gift or equipping gift" ministry as an apostle, prophet, evangelist, pastor, or teacher. Perhaps you desperately need a miracle to recover the edge of God's anointing in your life. The Lord is ready to make the iron float. He wants to return the cutting edge to your ministry.

I was only able to take hold of God's best for me after I gave my church back to God! I had to apologize for all my manipulation and my attempts to out-perform and drive my people. Now it is God's church. If you know what you need to throw away, then throw it away. Empty your hands of your dead works using dead sticks—make room in your hands and heart for the new anointing that God has prepared for you.

Chapter 10

Pound the Ground

God is about to apprehend you for a divine destiny—and it's too late to think about escape, delay, or avoidance. You stepped across the line when you decided to read this book. Your apprehension and arrest is a burning desire in the heart of God. He has already bolted the doors and you can't get out without dealing with the entrustment of the One who made you. Of course, you may try to run nonetheless, but God will get you in the car parking lot if necessary.

You are not alone. Untold numbers of people in our "transition generation" have a divine appointment with a persistent God who loves us with a flaming passion. I am not talking about the salvation experience here, although it also is of eternal importance. I am talking about entering our destiny in God. When I encountered the fire of God's anointing—many years after I had been saved—it "ruined" me for life. I thought I would "plough" my particular field of ministry the same way people had been ploughing them for years. However, once God threw His mantle of renewal anointing and revival fire over my life, nothing else would do. I was too "ruined" to ever return to the usual methods and activities I used to enjoy in my Christian life and ministry. God lit a fire in Sunderland and then He asked me to throw my "instruments of field" into that fire.

Do you know what I pray for any church I visit now? "Lord, devastate it. Ruin it forever!" You may find this hard to believe, but there is a solid Bible precedent for this "ruining" quality of God's fiery anointing. Look closely at the biblical record of Elisha's call through Elijah the prophet in First Kings 19:

> So he departed from there, and found Elisha the son of Shaphat, who was plowing with twelve yoke of oxen before him, and he was with the twelfth. Then Elijah passed by him and **threw his mantle on him**. And he left the oxen and ran after Elijah, and said, "Please let me kiss my father and my mother, and then I will follow you." And he said to him, "Go back again, for what have I done to you?" So Elisha turned back from him, and took a yoke of oxen and slaughtered them and boiled their flesh, using the oxen's equipment, and gave it to the people, and they ate. Then he arose and followed Elijah, and became his servant (1 Kings 19:19-21).

Once Elijah covered Elisha with the mantle of his anointing, the man was "ruined for life." He would never again be fit for the fields of his father because he knew what it was like to bear the anointing of Almighty God on his shoulders—even if it was for only a moment of time. His transformation was so complete that he burned his bridges (or in this case, oxen and yokes) behind him. He could never return to life as usual. In fact, Elisha spent the rest of his life either serving Elijah and seeking to walk under that mantle again, or fulfilling his own entrustment after he had received a double anointing from God. From the first day he left the fields onward, Elisha was engaged in an adventure of surprise, faith, and miracles. He was used by God again and again to confront men with choices that demanded responses of faith.

It's Your Choice

Elisha had become sick with the illness of which he would die. Then Joash the king of Israel came down to him, and wept over his face, and said, "O my father, my father, the chariots of Israel and their horsemen!" And Elisha said to him, "Take a bow and some arrows." So he took himself a bow and some arrows. Then he said to the king of Israel, "Put your hand on the bow." So he put his hand on it, and Elisha put his hands on the king's hands. And he said, "Open the east window"; and he opened it. Then Elisha said, "Shoot"; and he shot. And he said, "The arrow of the Lord's deliverance and the arrow of deliverance from Syria; for you must strike the Syrians at Aphek till you have destroyed them" (2 Kings 13:14-17).

Did you notice that after Elisha told King Joash to pick up a bow and arrows, the Bible says "Elisha put his hands on the king's hands" (2 Kings 13:16b). What does that mean to you? (I've really studied the original Hebrew in this passage, and I've concluded that Elisha stood behind the king and put his arms around him to put his hands on the king's hands. King Joash was cloaked in the prophetic. If Elisha had positioned himself in front of King Joash, he would have been shot through the chest.) Then the prophet told Joash to open the east window and shoot the arrow. What the prophet says next is crucial to properly understanding the verse that follows. Elisha told King Joash in plain terms, "The arrow of the Lord's deliverance and the arrow of deliverance from

Syria; for you must strike the Syrians at Aphek *till you have destroyed them*" (2 Kings 13:17b). Now look at what happened:

*Then he said, "Take the arrows"; so he took them. And he said to the king of Israel, "Strike the ground"; so **he struck three times, and stopped**. And the man of God was angry with him, and said, "**You should have struck five or six times; then you would have struck Syria till you had destroyed it!** But now you will strike Syria only three times"* *(2 Kings 13:18-19).*

Your life in God didn't begin and end the day you received Jesus Christ as Lord and Savior. It only began a process in which every day presents a cross for you to take up before you follow Him anew. Maturity and fruitfulness come through everyday obedience and sacrifices of comfort, self-reliance, and self-centeredness. That is why God isn't content with only our decision to leave our field of comfort. He wants us to burn our instruments of self-maintenance behind us. He isn't satisfied if we obey a command to pick up a bow and arrows. He wants us to go on and open the east window—even if it seems silly. He wants us to submit to the guiding hands of others from time to time, who help us fire arrows into thin air for reasons we don't fully comprehend. But it gets worse.

God wants us to take *hold* of the rest of His prophetic arrows and start striking the ground. He wants proof that we won't give up. Will we be like King Joash who struck the ground only three times, or will we persistently pound the ground for total victory—even when the revival seems to get "out of hand" a little bit? Can we stand in the fire of God even when it's unpredictable and seemingly uncontrollable? God wants to raise up a generation of priests and kings who will strike the ground with His anointing and promises until it hurts the enemy where it counts. For decades the Church has been content to strike the ground three times and then pull back—fearing that "wild fire" would break out. Unfortunately, half-way commitment always produces half-way results.

Think of Jacob who wrestled with the angel of the Lord until daybreak. Jacob refused to let go of his destiny in God. Are you willing to declare, "I'm not going to let go! Even if it's painful, even if I am in agony and my hip joint is out of joint, I refuse to give in to the temptation to let go and give up." God may ask you, "Do you want to give in? Do you want to stop now?" but He really wants to hear you say, "No! I won't let go until You bless me."

You are reading the final pages of the final chapter in this book because you have refused to give up! You weren't prepared to give up in Chapters 1, or 2, or 5, or even Chapter 9. Your time has come. The arrows of God are in your hand, and the choice is yours. Will you pound the ground with those arrows until the obstacles of the enemy totally shatter? Will you shout loud enough and long enough for God to hear you and stop where you are?

You will never defeat your spiritual Syria by merely firing arrows out of windows. The fact that someone anoints your forehead with some olive oil does nothing if you measure the amount of power in the oil itself. These things are *symbols* of powerful truths in God, and the Bible is full of them. Whether God tells you to dip yourself seven times under the muddy waters of the River Jordan or just spits in your face, the healing anointing comes through your obedience—not through the muddy water or spit. You may need to shout to God right now, although the shout will do nothing to stop God through its measurable volume. The fact is that

God will be arrested by the shout in your heart. He is stopped in His tracks when He notices a "shout that He can't ignore." When He sees and hears people of passion crying out to Him for more of His presence and glory, He declares in the heavens, "These people are taking their window of opportunity. I have got to respond to them; I must visit their homes and churches. I will come to them Myself."

Leave the Field, Seize the Mantle

I believe that everyone who leaves all to follow God will live an "Elisha life" in one form or another from the first day they leave their fields by faith. Some will experience the adventure of Elijah in a divine appointment when they cast their mantle on others and see them respond to God by leaving their own fields. Lois and I found ourselves being challenged by God to "pound the ground" for total victory in our areas of entrustment. Would we only strike the ground three times, or would we pound the ground and fire the arrows for total victory?

After God spoke to me about my failure to honor my entrustment for the local neighborhood, I reluctantly accepted God's request to turn over the building to the community. But I had no idea how we were going to finally reach out to the neighborhood we had neglected for two years. We didn't know it at the time, but God had honored our obedience and He was about to provide us with a new "Elisha" from the very fields we had been sent to harvest. This young Elisha was one of the keys to breakthrough in fulfilling and expanding our entrustment to bring the life of God to East Sunderland!

One night during a renewal service in Sunderland, I saw two young women lying on the floor after they received ministry. The power of God was all over them, and the manifestations of His power were so obvious that I asked one of the elders, "Who are these young ladies?" He said, "They are Catholic girls who go to mass every Sunday morning. They said they came to our renewal meetings because 'God is in this place.' "

We didn't realize that these two ladies were sisters, and that one of them was living with one of the most notorious and feared gangsters in the area. This man ran prostitution and drug rings, handled underworld enforcement contracts, and masterminded protection and racketeering operations in two major cities. (These involved intimidating individuals and businesses to pay high fees for "protection" services. If the would-be clients refused, he would quickly inflict his own brand of violence on them.) He was interested in anything that could make him money. He was widely feared as a man of extreme violence. He was a huge man who had won an amateur weight lifting title in Great Britain.

Two weeks after the sisters were touched by God in our meetings, the gangster asked the one who was living with him, "What are you doing every night?" When she said, "I'm going to church," he bluntly answered, "I don't want you to go anymore."

"I can't stop going," she said. "Listen," he answered, "they're brainwashing you. There's no God, and there's no power! What are you doing this for? You're ruining my life." She wouldn't budge. She said, "I can't stop going. You need to come," but he just shook his head and said, "I would never go there." But then, almost in the same breath, he told her, "Tell me about it."

"Well, there's about 800 people turn up every night, and the cars are parked all..." she began, but he suddenly interrupted her, and there was a wicked gleam in his eye. "These cars that are parked—how do they look after them during the services?" When she said, "They have a security firm," he told her, "I'm coming down."

The sudden reversal of attitudes had one motive behind it—the love of money. He thought that he could intimidate the security firms handling our building and parking lot security and extort some protection money from them on the side. That was how this man made his way into our renewal services one Friday night. He managed to sit emotionless through the worship time, but as soon as it was over, this hulking giant of a man literally got up from his seat and ran all the way home. It was the only thing he knew to do to help him deal with something that was overwhelming. He had just had an encounter with Someone who was infinitely more powerful than he was.

By the time the girl came home at around midnight that night, she found him sitting alone in his living room in total darkness. "What are you doing?" she asked. "Nothing," he said. "Why are you sitting here with the lights off? You never do that." He said, "Well, I'm doing that tonight."

She said, "Something is wrong with you." At first he wouldn't respond, but she kept after him until he finally said, "Okay, I ran home because there's something in that place that I didn't like! And I don't want you to go back ever again!"

She knew she had him, and she kept working on him from morning until night to return to the renewal meetings. Eventually he said, "Okay, listen, *I'll come one more time, and I'm going to put this matter to rest*! I'm going to expose that preacher for what he is, right in front of everybody." The girl took those arrows of opportunity and struck the ground a few more times. "That's okay, fine. Now you know the real reason why you don't want to come, don't you? *You're afraid*."

That was his ultimate hot button and raw nerve. "Listen to me," he said. "I'm frightened of neither man nor beast, and I'll be there!" He showed up true to his word too. He sat through the worship, and he sat through my entire message. When it was time for me to make an appeal, I felt impressed to make a call for salvation. I said, "Those who want to get saved, put your hand up." His hand shot into the air, and he told us later that he kept looking at his hand like it had a mind of its own.

Like any good Pentecostal preacher, I saw his hand long before he managed to pull it back and stick it in a pocket. It was about to get worse for him, because I said, "All those who have raised their hand, come to the front."

He was thinking, *Now is my chance. When I get to the front, I'm going to tell this guy what he is. I'm going to expose him in front of everybody*. He told me later that if I had argued with him, he planned to punch me right in front of everyone. (I'm glad I didn't argue with him.)

I remember watching this huge hulk of a man walking down to the front, and he had a peculiar look on his face. In that moment, the Spirit of God spoke to me. I pointed my finger at him and said, "This man wants to get saved!" As soon I did that, the power of God hit him like a heavyweight fighter landing a sucker punch. I saw this huge man rock back and forth like a drunken man, and then he fell to the floor. He struggled to come back up to a sitting position and then steadied himself. While he was still rocking back and forth, the Lord hit him again and he found himself flat on his back.

I watched him try to get up, and it looked like he was pinned to the ground by an unseen hand (he was). This man was pinned to the floor for 15 minutes before he finally managed to get up, but when he stood up with tears streaming down his face, I could see that his eyes were crystal clear. His face had been transformed. All that bottled-up anger and violence had been visibly stripped away, and we had seen a "Saul of Tarsus conversion" take place right in front of us. No one was more thrilled than the girl, who watched the whole miracle take place right in front of her eyes. When I asked him what happened, this is what he said:

"Well, I wanted to get up. I'm a street fighter, and the last place I wanted to be was on my back among people I didn't know. My instinct told me, 'Get up, get up!' and I was trying to get up, but it was like this hand was on my chest, and it just kept me down. Then I heard something like a voice saying, *'Why don't you just surrender?'* And do you know what? I thought, *I think I will.*

"Even though I was the man behind most of the drugs, the prostitution, the violence, and everything else going on in the area, I still lived under the constant pressure of fear. I didn't know if I was going to get shot or get killed that night. I didn't know who my friends were or who my enemies were—so I wouldn't trust anybody. I never knew when the police would come for me at 2:00 or 3:00 in the morning all tooled up with their guns. Really, I was ready to give up. I was ready to surrender."

He surrendered to the Lord that night, and when he got up off that floor, he walked away from his life as a career criminal and underworld figure. He knew it would cost him something, but all he could do was follow Jesus and leave the details to Him. He and the girl were married shortly after he came to Christ. At the time of this writing, this young Elisha and his wife—themselves products of the street—are working with street kids in another country, away from threats of violence.

Sometimes We Don't Recognize Him

King Joash failed to pound the ground until he had total victory over Syria because he didn't recognize the form or look of God's deliverance. Perhaps he expected to see the fire come down as it had in Elijah's ministry. Maybe he expected to see angels come down and suddenly destroy his enemies, or a sudden rainstorm come out of nowhere. That's the way things happened in the past, but this pounding the ground business just didn't seem normal. Why would he, the king of Israel, have to go out in public in broad daylight and pound arrows into the ground. Everyone would think he had gone mad, or senile at best. He was probably thinking, *If you ask me, this Elisha character is missing a few marbles here. It's obvious he is about to die. I'll just hit the ground a few times to satisfy him so he won't get any stranger.*

Many people around the world are in danger of missing God's deliverance for their churches, communities, and nations because they don't recognize God in this current renewal and revival. It doesn't seem to match their familiar ways and patterns of the past, so they are tempted to throw it all out as emotional outbursts by unstable people, or as demonic frauds created by evil men.

The Bible tells us in Matthew 14 that Jesus went to a mountain to pray while His disciples crossed the Sea of Galilee in a boat. Most of the disciples were seasoned fishermen who had made their living on that lake, but by late evening they were in trouble. They had reached the middle of the sea when a "contrary wind" blew up a dangerous storm with high waves (see Mt. 14:23-25). Jesus went out to them walking on the water. I want you to imagine how the disciples in the boat felt. They knew they were in serious trouble. The waves were coming into the boat, and Jesus was far away from them somewhere on a mountain. Then one of the disciples yelled out in fear, "What's that walking on the water?!" Have *you* ever seen anything walk on water? Neither had they.

> *And when the disciples saw Him walking on the sea, they were troubled, saying, "It is a ghost!" And they cried out for fear. But immediately Jesus spoke to them, saying, "Be of good cheer! It is I; do not be afraid." And Peter answered Him and said, "Lord, if it is You, command me to come to You on the water." So He said, "Come." And when Peter had come down out of the boat, he walked on the water to go to Jesus. But when he saw that the wind was boisterous, he was afraid; and beginning to sink he cried out, saying, "Lord, save me!" And immediately Jesus stretched out His hand and caught him, and said to him, "O you of little faith, why did you doubt?" And when they got into the boat, the wind ceased. Then those who were in the boat came and worshiped Him, saying, "Truly You are the Son of God" (Matthew 14:26-33).*

When the disciples first saw their Deliverer and the answer to their prayers, they all thought they were seeing a ghost, not their familiar Jesus. They all shouted out, "A-G-H-H-H-H!" One thing I'm sure of is that none of them shouted, "Hallelujah!" Those men shouted out of fear because they didn't see Jesus; they thought they saw a *ghost*. What were their options here? Look at their circumstances.

They could give the ghost a shout, or they could drown in the boat. Those were their choices. All they knew was that this ghost-like thing was walking right past them—and that is not normal. The only one they *knew* was capable of such a thing was Jesus, but they had never seen Him do such a thing before. What if it was Him? Someone probably said, "Well, it doesn't *look like* Him. No, it just doesn't look like Jesus." I think Peter reasoned, *Well, we're going to drown if it isn't Him. So I think that the ghost is worth a shout!*

What If It's Jesus?

For many people, this move of God is the most ghost-like thing they've ever seen. It cuts right across the grain of their church traditions. Unless you've read Church history, you have probably never seen or heard of anything quite like this current move of God—it's positively ghost-like. If you are in this position today, then I urge you to look at your circumstances. You are sinking in a boat that is about to be swamped in waves of apathy, powerless traditions, and human politics. That's not much of an option. This ghost-like thing is worth a shout! After all, *what if it is Jesus?*

I have to warn you that if you dare to shout to God in your storm, then things will seem to get worse before they get better! Look at what happened to Peter. As soon as someone on the sinking boat got up enough courage to shout to the "ghost," the ghost answered back! Then Peter just had to challenge the ghost by saying, "If it is *really* You, Jesus, then command me [notice that Peter didn't say 'ask me'] to come out to You." And that is just what Jesus did. He'll do the same to you today!

You need to understand that you will never discern whether or not this move is of God with your natural eyes. Every disciple in that boat was convinced by their natural eyes that they were seeing a ghost, not Jesus Christ. And every one of them was wrong. Finally one of them dared to give the ghost a shout. Even as Peter was filling his lungs to shout to the ghost, he was probably thinking, *My mind just can't cope with this.* Honestly, my friend, your mind can't cope with this either, and it never will. *It never will.* No one on that boat realized he was looking at Jesus walking on the water until the moment He said, "Fear not, it is I." They didn't know what they were seeing with their natural eyes. No matter how hard they stared or how critically they examined the evidence, they couldn't discern His form or shape—*but they knew His voice.*

Throughout this renewal and revival, I've seen a lot of things that I don't understand and I can't discern. But all along the way, I've heard the familiar and reassuring voice of the Lord saying, "Ken, fear not. Ken, fear not. It's Me. It's Me." I know His voice because the Bible says, "My sheep know My voice" (see Jn. 10:3-4). I've walked with God for more than four decades, and I'm a third-generation Pentecostal Assemblies of God minister. I know when God speaks to me. I know His voice, my friend. I've heard it from my first days as a little boy in His house. That is why, when God spoke to me in that very unfamiliar and strange ministry setting in Holy Trinity Anglican Church at Brompton, I felt peace. He told me, "Don't worry, Ken, this is Me." I relaxed and yielded to His Spirit because I recognized His voice.

Once you shout to the voice you recognize in the midst of the storm, don't be surprised when He commands you to step out of your familiar boat to meet Him on the waters of uncertainty. I don't think we'll ever understand it logically, but we will hear Him constantly reassure us, "Fear not; it is I." Your only response is to say, "Yes." When you dare to step out by faith, He will be there for you—even if you sink from time to time. In the end, He will step back into the boat with you and bring total calm to the sea.

These are crucial times when you need Jesus in your boat in the midst of the sea. You don't need the Jesus in the manger, and you don't need the Jesus of your tradition. You don't even need the Jesus that you perceive in your mind. You probably need the Jesus who appears to be so ghost-like in the middle of transition, in the middle of the stormy seas of true confrontational revival in the Church. Don't fear the ghost on your stormy sea; it's probably the very Jesus you need in your boat. Let Him cut through the offense and step into your boat to touch you.

God is moving in virtually every continent and nation on earth today. Souls are being swept into the Kingdom of God by the thousands and millions, not by the mere hundreds. Never have we seen the winds of revival stirring as they are today. We all face a decision. The outward manifestation or appearance of God's outpouring to a Church adrift in a troubled sea of empty religion and corrupt society may seem more annoying and frightening than anointed—but what voice do we hear calling out to our hearts, *"Fear not, it is I"*?

If it really is Jesus Christ come to us in a fresh form and shape, do we dare turn away from Him in fear? What if this renewal and revival is the genuine forerunner of another, even greater awakening in the earth? Who among us wants to take the "credit" for calling God a ghost and dismissing Him as a demonic apparition just because He chose to come to us in a different form than what we are used to?

What if the fire, the passion, and the power of this move of God today are His arrows of deliverance in our hand?

What if He wants us to pound the ground with His arrows until we see the knowledge of His glory cover the earth? I don't want to timidly hit the earth three times and then draw back in doubt and unbelief or embarrassment. If you hear God's reassuring voice saying, "Fear not, it is I," then seize the arrows of opportunity and pound the ground until the gates of hell give way! There is revival in the land and no one can stop the King of glory!

Destiny Image
New Releases

IN SEARCH OF REVIVAL
by Stuart Bell.

Will revival always look the same? Who will recognize it when it comes? What part do we play in bringing revival to our areas? How do we sustain revival? *In Search of Revival* details how you can position yourself for the moving of God's Spirit. You'll see characteristics marking churches on their own quest. Get ready to see revival in a whole new way!

Paperback Book, 176p. ISBN 0-7684-1001-0 Retail $9.99

USER FRIENDLY PROPHECY
by Larry J. Randolph.

Hey! Now you can learn the basics of prophecy and how to prophesy in a book that's written for you! Whether you're a novice or a seasoned believer, this book will stir up the prophetic gift God placed inside you and encourage you to step out in it.

Paperback Book, 208p. ISBN 1-56043-695-6 Retail $9.99

THE LOST ART OF INTERCESSION
by Jim W. Goll.

How can you experience God's anointing power as a result of your own prayer? Learn what the Moravians discovered during their 100-year prayer Watch. They sent up prayers; God sent down His power. Jim Goll, who ministers worldwide through a teaching and prophetic ministry, urges us to heed Jesus' warning to "watch." Through Scripture, the Moravian example, and his own prayer life, Jim Goll proves that "what goes up must come down."

Paperback Book, 182p. ISBN 1-56043-697-2 Retail $9.99

FLASHPOINTS OF REVIVAL
by Geoff Waugh.

Throughout history, revival has come to various countries and peoples. Why those times? Why those people? Why not others? This book takes you inside the hearts and minds of people who lived through the major revivals of the past years. Discover how today's revivals fit into God's timeline of awakenings.

Paperback Book, 192p. ISBN 0-7684-1002-9 Retail $9.99

Available at your local Christian bookstore.
Internet: http://www.reapernet.com

Prices subject to change without notice.

Destiny Image
Revival Books

LET NO ONE DECEIVE YOU
by Dr. Michael L. Brown.
No one is knowingly deceived. Everyone assumes it's "the other guy" who is off track. So when people dispute the validity of current revivals, how do you know who is right? In this book Dr. Michael Brown takes a look at current revivals and at the arguments critics are using to question their validity. After examining Scripture, historical accounts of past revivals, and the fruits of the current movements, Dr. Brown comes to a logical conclusion: God's Spirit is moving. *Let No One Deceive You!*
Paperback Book, 320p. ISBN 1-56043-693-X (6" X 9") Retail $10.99

THE GOD MOCKERS
And Other Messages From the Brownsville Revival
by Stephen Hill.
Hear the truth of God as few men have dared to tell it! In his usual passionate and direct manner, Evangelist Stephen Hill directs people to an uncompromised Christian life of holiness. The messages in this book will burn through every hindrance that keeps you from going further in God!
Paperback Book, 182p. ISBN 1-56043-691-3 Retail $9.99

IT'S TIME
by Richard Crisco.
"We say that 'Generation X' does not know what they are searching for in life. But we are wrong. They know what they desire. We, as the Church, are the ones without a revelation of what they need." It is time to stop entertaining our youth with pizza parties and start training an army for God. Find out in this dynamic book how the Brownsville youth have exploded with revival power...affecting the surrounding schools and communities!
Paperback Book, 144p. ISBN 1-56043-690-5 Retail $9.99

A TOUCH OF GLORY
by Lindell Cooley.
This book was written for the countless "unknowns" who, like Lindell Cooley, are being plucked from obscurity for a divine work of destiny. Here Lindell, the worship leader of the Brownsville Revival, tells of his own journey from knowing God's hand was upon him to trusting Him. The key to personal revival is a life-changing encounter with the living God. There is no substitute for a touch of His glory.
Paperback Book, 182p. ISBN 1-56043-689-1 Retail $9.99

Available at your local Christian bookstore.
Internet: http://www.reapernet.com

Prices subject to change without notice.